Exploring
Questions
in RE

CARYS THOMAS

VICKY THOMAS

SERIES EDITOR
GRAHAM DAVIES

1

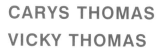

Published in 2005 by:
Nelson Thornes Ltd
Delta Place
27 Bath Road
CHELTENHAM
GL53 7TH
United Kingdom

05 06 07 08 09 / 10 9 8 7 6 5 4 3 2 1

A catalogue record for this book is available from the British Library

ISBN 0 7487 9362 3
Illustrations by Rupert Besley, Angela Lumley and Richard Morris
Picture research by Sue Sharp
Edited by Melanie Gray
Page make-up by DP Press Ltd

Printed in Croatia by Zrinski

Acknowledgements
With thanks to the following for permission to reproduce photographs and other copyright material in this book:
Alamy/ A Room With Views: 37 (top right); Alamy/ Christa Stadtler: 37 (middle right); Alamy/ Janine Wiedel Photo Library: 37 (bottom right); Alamy/ Jeff Greenberg: 91 (B); Alamy/ Norma Joseph: 66; Alamy/ Photofusion: 17 (top), 78 (top); Alamy/ Terrance Klassen: 19 (middle right); Alamy/ World Religions Photo Library: 18 (top left), 19 (middle left), 41 (top left), 53 (G); Andes Press Agency/ Carlos Reyes-Manzo: 11 (top right), 19 (bottom), 25, 41 (all except top left), 42 (bottom right), 52 (C), 53 (H), 63 (H), 84 (F), 88 (A&B); ArkReligion.com/Ester James: 84 (C, D, E&G); Art Directors & Trip Photo Library/ www.arkreligion.com: 10 (bottom left), 11 (top middle), 14, 18 (middle and bottom left), 19 (top middle and right), 37 (bottom left), 48 (all), 71 (middle right), 83; John Birdsall Social Issues Photo Library: 39 (top left), 45 (top), 46 (bottom right), 57, 71 (bottom), 87 (bottom), 88 (top right); Brand X RW (NT): 51 (B), 52 (D); Bridgeman Art Library: 27 (top); Circa Photo Library: 12, 17 (bottom), 18 (top right and bottom right), 19 (top left); Circa Photo Library/ John Smith: 52 (top); Circa Photo Library/ Mike Edwards: 27 (bottom); Circa Photo Library/ William Holtby: 33 (right), 42 (bottom left); Corbis/ David H Wells: 71 (middle left); Corbis/ Kevin R Morris: 91 (E); Corbis/ Paul A Souders: 11 (top left); Corbis/ Reuters: 18 (middle right); Corbis/S.I.N.: 70; Corel 76 (NT): 46 (top left); Corel 162 (NT): 51 (E); Corel 186 (NT): 51 (G); Corel 248 (NT):87 (C bottom); Corel 307 (NT): 45; Corel 414 (NT): 63 (E); Corel 511 (NT): 53 (J); Corel 588 (NT): 63 (F); Corel 606 (NT): 44 (bottom); Corel 641 (NT): 46 (bottom); Graham Davies: 42 (top), 43 (both), 44 (A&C), 67; Digital Stock 4 (NT): 34 (right); Digital Stock 11 (NT): 53 (F); Digital Vision 7 (NT): 73; Empics/ PA/ Ian Nicholson: 89; Image 100 22 (NT): 62 (C); Ingram V2 CD4 (NT): 78 (C); Israel Images: 82 (top, middle right and bottom); Sujatin Johnson: 33 (left); Father Peter Murray s.m., Roman Catholic National Shrine, Walsingham: 51 (F); Muslim Aid UK: 53 (E); Offside Sports Photography: 37 (top left), 46 (bottom left), 76; Photodisc 16 (NT): 40, 79; Photodisc 19 (NT): 62 (D), 87 (C top); Photodisc 32 (NT): 39 (top right), 51 (D), 62 (A&B); Photodisc 54 (NT): 65; Photodisc 75 (NT): 37 (H); Photofusion: 47 (top); Photolibrary Wales/ Steve Benbow: 8 (all), 10 (all except bottom left), 38 (both), 39 (left); Rosie Pratt: 51 (A); Press Association/ Barry Batchelor: 23; Press Association/ David Jones: 53 (I); Red Cross: 52 (B), 78 (E); Rex Features/ James D Morgan: 46 (middle); Rex Features/ Oleg Konin: 32; Rex Features/ Paul Felix: 47 (bottom); The Smiles Foundation: 71 (top); STP/Martin Sookias: 29; Tearfund: 11 (I); Throssel Hole Buddhist Abbey: 11 (H); Gary Thomas c/o Dylan Thomas Theatre, Swansea www.dylanthomastheatre.org.uk: 34 (left); World Religions Photo Library www.worldreligions.co.uk: 16, 86; World Religions Photo Library/Christine Osborne: 84 (B).

Every effort has been made to contact copyright holders. The publishers apologise to anyone whose rights have been inadvertently overlooked, and will be happy to rectify any errors or omissions.

Contents

Introduction

We want you to be an excellent learner

In this book you will explore lots of questions about life and religion. This will involve finding out about beliefs and practices, ceremonies and rituals, as well as considering what members of faith communities think about those questions.

The questions aim to get you thinking about your own experiences of life, and help you to examine your feelings, values and beliefs. You will be encouraged to respond in your own words to pictures, questions and activities, sharing your views with others in your class. You will be able to listen to the opinions of others and to move forward in developing your own views and opinions.

We want you to be an excellent thinker

To be an excellent thinker, you need to:

- have a critical attitude to all the information you read. Never take anything for granted – question it
- keep an open mind – don't close down the possibilities too early
- ask lots of 'why' questions – try to work out the reasons for an action or viewpoint
- think about your thinking – give yourself some time to reflect on what you have read or discussed
- talk about your thinking – put your views into words. Listen carefully to the opinions of others and consider whether you need to adapt your view as a result
- look for connections between what you are learning now and what you have already learned. Try to see links with other religions or viewpoints.

We want you to develop these skills

We want you to develop these skills
- **Analysing what you are learning**: this might involve seeing patterns, organising different parts, making connections, making comparisons, explaining and interpreting.
- **Applying knowledge and understanding**: you can do this in a number of ways. For example, you might demonstrate, illustrate, modify and classify.
- **Empathy:** this involves being sensitive to the feelings and beliefs of others in the group. Put yourself in other people's shoes and see the world from their point of view.

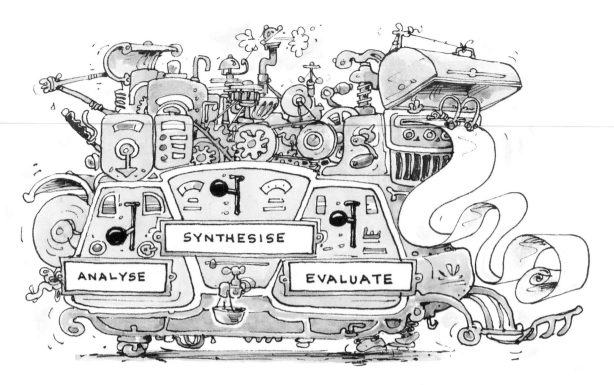

ANALYSE   SYNTHESISE   EVALUATE

We want you to develop these skills too...

- **Enquiry**: you will need to research, investigate, observe and gather information from a number of sources, including books, sacred texts, CD-ROMs and websites.
- **Evaluation**: when you evaluate you make a judgement about how valuable, useful, accurate or meaningful something is. You might be putting something to the test, comparing ideas and making a decision about it.
- **Listening**: be an active listener. Focus on the person who is speaking and make some response either in your own mind or out loud to what is being said.
- **Making decisions**: to make meaningful decisions demands rigorous information gathering, careful consideration of the options, weighing up the advantages and disadvantages, deciding on the action and evaluating the outcomes.

- **Problem-solving**: you need to be able to tackle issues and problems, examine the evidence, look at the different possibilities, test solutions and come to conclusions.
- **Reasoning**: this is about giving reasons for opinions and actions, and making judgements and decisions informed by reasons or evidence.
- **Reflection**: this is an opportunity to consider what you have learned, examine your inner feelings, and consider some of the deeper questions of life. Other skills of being still and meditating are part of this.
- **Skills of synthesis**: this means bringing together and relating knowledge and understanding from different areas of study, drawing conclusions, and building on what you know to think of new ideas.

This book will give you lots of opportunities to use and develop these skills as you read, discuss and engage in the variety of activities.

We wish you 'good thinking'!

Who am I?

This is about ...

- **Exploring who you are and recognising what influences you**
- **Considering the communities you belong to and how they influence you**
- **Learning about religious communities and some of their customs, beliefs and practices**
- **Asking questions and expressing opinions**

Key questions

- **Who am I?**
- **What am I like?**
- **What makes me like I am?**

What influences me?

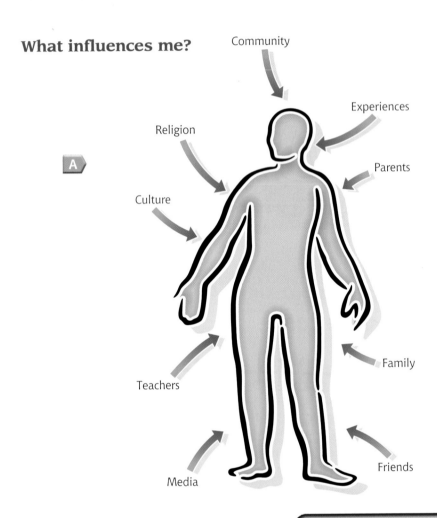

A

Congratulations! You have just started your new secondary school.

For many pupils this is a big step and you might be feeling different emotions, like excitement and nervousness. During this time you will meet new people and make new friends. You may meet people who have quite different cultural and religious backgrounds from yours. They may have beliefs that are different from your own. Valuing these differences is an important part of what RE is about.

Recall ...

You studied RE at your primary school. Which religions did you learn about?

KEY WORDS

- Beliefs
- Community
- Customs
- Practices

In your RE lessons you will learn about what people believe and do. You will also ask questions, learn from your own experiences and those of others. Some of these questions are to do with your personal identity – how you see yourself – and they include:

- who am I?
- what am I like?
- what makes me like I am?

1 Think about the different roles or relationships you have with others.

  a Create a spider diagram to show these relationships.

  b Which of these relationships are most important to you? Write these under your diagram.

  c Explain your choices.

2 On a piece of paper, write your name and one thing about yourself that your classmates might not know about you. Fold the paper in half to hide what you have written. Hand it to your teacher. Your teacher will then choose some to read out to the class, so be ready to tell everyone a bit more about yourself!

In my spare time I'm a mud-wrestler.

3 What are the things that influence you as a person? Look at picture **A** on the opposite page for some ideas.

  a Using a diamond nine template, put in order of importance the nine things that influence you.

  b Compare your diagram with a partner and discuss your top three choices.

  c Write a short description of the things that most influence you and explain why.

4 Have you seen the television programme *Friends*? In this programme, friendship is the most important thing in life for the six main characters. Their friends have a big influence on who they are. How do you deal with friends who want to change you into what they want you to be, or who want you to do something you don't want to do?

  a Write an example (it can be made up) of when friends put pressure on you to do something you don't want to do.

  b Write a list of ways you could resist this pressure.

  c Think of all the ways in which you can influence your friends, and write a list of as many as you can think of.

OVER TO YOU

Let's reflect

'Friends are like a box of chocolates. It is the inside that counts.'

What do you think about this statement?

Where do I belong?

This is about ...

- **Thinking about the communities you belong to**
- **Making comparisons between different communities**

Key questions

- Why do people belong to a **community**?
- Why are **symbols** of belonging important?

Gareth and Claire are penpals. They have just started at their new secondary schools. Here are some pictures of their two schools. Look at the pictures carefully, and then answer the questions that follow them.

School B

School A

KEY WORDS

- **Community**
- **Customs**
- **Muhammad**
- **Prophet**
- **Rules**
- **Symbols**

1 Look carefully at the photos of the two schools.

   a What are the similarities and differences?

   b Is one of them similar to your school? Explain your answer.

2 Read the emails in box **F**.

   a Gareth says he felt nervous when he started at his secondary school, and Claire says she was excited. Describe how you felt when you started at your school.

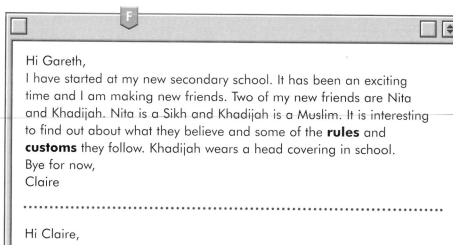

Hi Gareth,
I have started at my new secondary school. It has been an exciting time and I am making new friends. Two of my new friends are Nita and Khadijah. Nita is a Sikh and Khadijah is a Muslim. It is interesting to find out about what they believe and some of the **rules** and **customs** they follow. Khadijah wears a head covering in school.
Bye for now,
Claire

Hi Claire,
I have also just started at secondary school. On the first day I was nervous but my friends from primary school were in the same class and this made me feel better. We enjoyed getting lost around the school. We often arrived late for lessons and the teachers didn't tell us off because it was our first week. I think they will be stricter next week! In RE lessons we have started to learn about people who belong to different faiths. We are studying Judaism and Islam. Unlike you, we don't have anyone from different faiths in our school. It must be great for you to be able to talk to your new friends Nita and Khadijah about what they believe. In my RE lessons I have learnt that Khadijah was the name of **Prophet Muhammad**'s wife. Can you ask your friend if this is true?
Speak to you soon,
Gareth

School is an important community that you belong to. There are also a number of other communities that people belong to.

Look at diagram **G**. It shows the different communities that Claire, Nita and Khadijah belong to. Then answer the questions alongside.

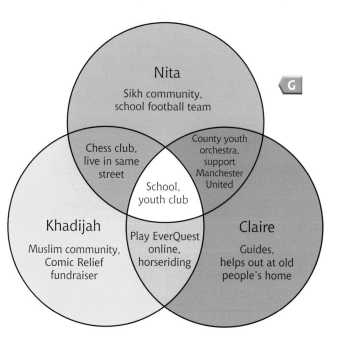

What's good about belonging to a community?

a Think about some of the communities you belong to and list what you like about being a member of them.
b How could you recognise that someone belongs to one of your communities?
c Are there any communities you would like to belong to? What would you need to do to be accepted?

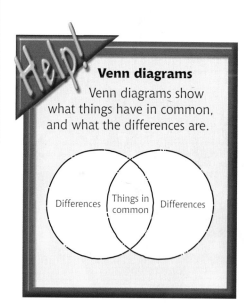

Venn diagrams
Venn diagrams show what things have in common, and what the differences are.

3 Diagrams like diagram **G** are called Venn diagrams. They show what things have in common.

a Looking at the diagram, what are the different communities that Claire, Nita and Khadijah each belong to?
b Which ones do they all belong to?

4 a List the communities that you belong to.
b In groups of two or three, draw a Venn diagram to show the communities you belong to.
c Which ones do you all have in common?

9

Where will I find religion in the community?

This is about ...

- Exploring your local community
- Analysing evidence of religion in your community

Look around your local area. What evidence can you see of religion in it? Have you noticed that not all religions are the same? People from different religions often have different and distinct **customs**, **beliefs** and **practices**. Sometimes people from the same religion also have some differences between themselves in the way they practise their religion. We call this **diversity**.

Key questions

- What is diversity?
- Is it good to have diversity in **communities**?
- How are communities changing?

KEY WORDS

- Beliefs
- Community
- Customs
- Diversity
- Practices

1 What evidence of religion in the community can you find in this collage of pictures? Do you know what religion each picture relates to? Find out about any picture you are not sure about.

2 **a** Think about your journey to school. Make a note of anything you see that has a connection to religion.

   b Look again at the photos on these pages. How do they help you to understand religious diversity?

'We are not all the same.'

'We speak different languages.'

'We come from different cultures.'

'We keep different traditions.'

Do you think diversity, as expressed in these statements, is important?

You will find links for this topic at www.nelsonthornes.com/exploringre

3 Find out about religion in your local community. Use maps, directories, websites and census information to prepare a report. It would be great to find out whether there have been any changes to religion in your community over the years. You could ask your parents about this.

Why is joining the Christian community important for Christians? (1) Infant baptism

This is about ...

- Learning about the Christian ceremony of infant baptism
- Understanding the importance of the ceremony for some Christians today
- Reflecting on the kind of commitment shown by Christians

Key questions

- Why is **infant baptism** important for some Christians?
- How do religious people show **commitment?**

In order to thank God for the gift of their child, many Christians have a special **ceremony** to welcome their child into the religious community. This ceremony is called infant baptism, or **christening**. It is found in many **denominations**, including the Anglican Church, the Roman Catholic Church, the Orthodox Church, the Methodist Church and others.

KEY WORDS

- Ceremony
- Christening
- Commitment
- Confirmation
- Denomination
- Font
- Godparents
- Infant baptism
- Minister
- Symbol

A

OVER TO YOU

1. In pairs, look at photo **A**, which shows a christening. Using the information on these two pages:
   a. identify who the people are in the photo.
   b. work out what stage of the ceremony it shows.
   c. find any Christian **symbols** in the photo.

B

Infant baptism in the Anglican Church

Q: When does infant baptism take place?
A: The ceremony usually takes place when the baby is a few months old.

Q: Where does the ceremony take place?
A: The ceremony usually takes place in the church. The service is held around the **font**, which is a container of water that has been blessed.

Q: Who is present?
A: The baby, parents, **godparents**, **minister**, friends and family, and members of the religious community are usually present.

Q: What happens during infant baptism?
A: Parents and godparents introduce the baby to be baptised.
Parents and godparent make promises.
The baby's name is announced.
The symbol of the cross is outlined on the forehead of the child using water from the font.
A candle is sometimes given to parents and godparents.

Brain Stretcher

Many parents have their babies baptised in church even though they do not go to church or believe in God. Do you agree with this? Explain your answer.

Faith • Faith • Faith
CONNECTIONS

Investigate how the ceremony of infant baptism is practised in the Roman Catholic and Orthodox Churches. Are there any differences between the Anglican, Catholic and Orthodox Churches? Write a short report.

OVER TO YOU

2 Look at the infant baptism cards in **C**.

 a What do they tell you about the ceremony of infant baptism?
 b What messages about infant baptism do these cards show?
 c Which card do you prefer and why?
 d What symbols can you see on the cards and why are they there?

C

On your *Baby's Christening*

Christening Day!
Congratulations

On Your
Goddaughter's Christening

May your goddaughter be surrounded with tenderness and love
Safe in the gentle care
of blessings from above

My name is Geraint and I am proud to have been asked to be a godparent to my niece Siân. It is a big responsibility. I am a committed Christian and I promise to make sure that Siân grows up in the Christian faith. I also promise that she will follow and trust in God and his Son, Jesus Christ. I will make sure that Siân attends church regularly. When Siân is older I hope she will make these promises for herself during the ceremony of **confirmation**.

Geraint

OVER TO YOU

Let's reflect

Think about the promises Geraint has made as a godparent.

 a How easy do you think it will be to keep these promises? Explain your view.
 b Why do you think Siân's godparents hope she will make the promises for herself when she is older?
 c Is it a good idea for somebody to make promises on behalf of someone else? Explain your response.

WEBLINKS **You will find links for this topic at** www.nelsonthornes.com/exploringre

Why is joining the Christian community important for Christians? (2) Believers' baptism

This is about ...

- Learning about the Christian ceremony of believers' baptism
- Understanding the importance of the ceremony for some Christians today
- Reflecting on the kind of commitment shown by Christians

Key questions

- Why is **believers' baptism** important for some Christians?
- How do religious people show **commitment**?

In some Churches, for example the Baptist Church, Christians do not practise **infant baptism**. Members of these Churches believe people should understand what baptism means and what is involved in living a Christian life. So they prefer to baptise those who can make up their own minds.

Fantastic Facts

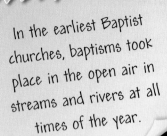

In the earliest Baptist churches, baptisms took place in the open air in streams and rivers at all times of the year.

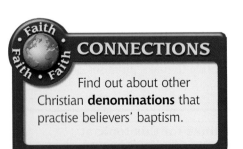

CONNECTIONS

Find out about other Christian **denominations** that practise believers' baptism.

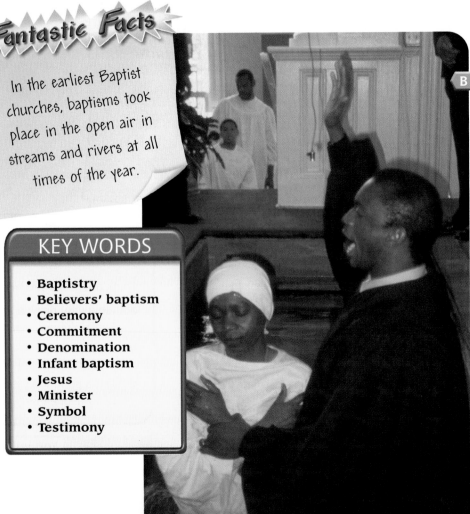

KEY WORDS

- Baptistry
- Believers' baptism
- Ceremony
- Commitment
- Denomination
- Infant baptism
- Jesus
- Minister
- Symbol
- Testimony

Believers' baptism in the Baptist Church

Q: When does the **ceremony** take place?
A: The ceremony usually takes place when the person is old enough to understand the significance of what they are doing.

Q: Where does the ceremony take place?
A: The ceremony usually takes place in the **baptistry** (a special pool) of the Baptist Church. However, some people are baptised in a stream, river, lake or in the sea because they remember that **Jesus** was baptised in the River Jordan.

Q: Who is present?
A: Friends, family and members of the congregation are usually present.

Q: Are there any preparations for the ceremony?
A: Yes, the candidate usually attends a number of classes with the **minister** or church leader in order to understand the significance of the ceremony. They study the Bible to understand what baptism means and what is involved in living a Christian life.

Q: What happens during believers' baptism?
A: The person being baptised usually wears white clothes as a symbol of being purified.
There will be singing and prayers.
The people who are to be baptised usually give a talk about how they became a Christian and why they are being baptised. This is called a **testimony**.
The candidate walks to the baptistry (or stream). The minister or church leader leads the person down a set of steps into the pool.
The person makes some promises – one of these will be to believe in Jesus Christ as Saviour and Lord.
The believer is totally immersed in the water. This symbolises the death of their old life and the start of a new one as a follower of Jesus Christ.
The person leaves the pool by another set of steps to show that they are now following a new path – a new life with Jesus.

Here is an example of a testimony from a young Baptist:

> Dear Lord,
>
> I stand before you today asking you to accept my testimony.
> I think of you as a loving father who will act as my guide in life.
> I know that I have not always behaved in the way that I should, that sometimes I have done things that are wrong. But I know that I want to change.
> I want to show everyone that I am a Christian and I want to be a good Christian. I know this will sometimes be hard, and that sometimes people won't understand why I want to be a Christian and may even tease me about it.
> But I ask you to help me and give me strength.
> I have learnt about Jesus being baptised in the River Jordan and I know you gave him the strength to carry on his work.
> I want to be baptised like Jesus and be cleansed of my wrongdoings.
> I promise to follow the example of Jesus.
> I promise to lead my life as you would want me to.

1 What happens before, during and after the ceremony of believers' baptism? List the main stages. Consider how the person being baptised may be feeling during these stages.

2 Design a **symbol** for believers' baptism to show its importance for believers.

3 Using a Venn diagram, record the similarities and differences between infant baptism and believers' baptism. (See page 94 for help with Venn diagrams.) You should include:

a the things that are only found in the ceremony of infant baptism.

b the things that are only found in the ceremony of believers' baptism.

c the things that are common to both infant baptism and believers' baptism.

Making a decision is the key part of believers' baptism. Do you think you should make the important decisions in your life, or are there times when other people should make them for you?

You will find links for this topic at
www.nelsonthornes.com/exploringre

Why is the amrit ceremony important for Sikhs?

This is about ...

- **Learning about the Sikh amrit ceremony**
- **Understanding the importance of the amrit ceremony for Sikhs today**
- **Reflecting on the kind of commitment shown by Sikhs**
- **Finding out more about the Sikh faith**

Key questions

- Why is the amrit ceremony important for Sikhs?
- How do religious people show **commitment**?

KEY WORDS

- **Amrit**
- **Ceremony**
- **Commitment**
- **Community**
- **Five Ks**
- **Gurdwara**
- **Guru Gobind Singh**
- **Guru Granth Sahib**
- **Khalsa**
- **Rules**

When people want to belong to the Sikh **community** and commit themselves to the Sikh way of life, they take part in the **amrit ceremony**.

This ceremony comes from the time of a great Sikh leader called **Guru Gobind Singh**, who chose five men who were willing to die for their faith. These men became the first members of the new Sikh community, called the **Khalsa** (the 'pure ones').

Today the amrit ceremony may take place at any age from adolescence up to adulthood. The person who wants to become a member of the Khalsa stands in front of five Khalsa members in the **gurdwara** and asks to be admitted to the faith. The amrit ceremony is a time for Sikhs to make serious promises for life and to keep the duties of every Sikh.

The most important part of the amrit ceremony is the drinking of amrit. Amrit is a mixture of sugar crystals and water. It is made in a steel bowl and stirred with a double-edged sword. The sword and bowl represent strength and firmness.

The five Khalsa members each take a turn at stirring the mixture and reading part of the **Guru Granth Sahib** (the Sikh holy book). The amrit mixture is sprinkled onto the hair and eyes of each person seeking to become a member of the Khalsa.

Fantastic Facts

Did you know that Sikhism is the youngest of the six world religions. It is 500 years old – that's young for a religion!

OVER TO YOU

1. Find out why amrit is:
   - **a** sprinkled on the eyes.
   - **b** sprinkled on the hair.

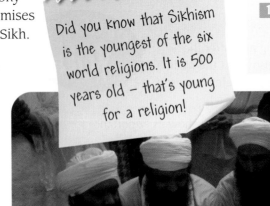

A

Jaswant

*I am 18 years old. I am a Sikh and I am seriously thinking about making a full commitment to my religion by taking amrit. Before I do this, I have to think very deeply about the promises I am going to make, because it means I will have to live strictly by the **rules** of my religion. If I take amrit, I become a member of the Khalsa. During the ceremony the rules I need to keep will be explained to me.*

Help!

Freeze frame

This involves setting up a scene as if it were a video freeze frame or a still from a movie. You need to choose a scene from the story and freeze it. You need to be able to describe how each character in the freeze frame is thinking and feeling at that precise moment.

OVER TO YOU

2 In pairs, discuss and explain why it is important for Jaswant to think seriously about making a commitment to his religion.

3 Look at the Khalsa rules.

   a Do you think they are fair rules?

   b Which rule would you find the easiest to keep? Explain why.

   c Which rule would be the most difficult to keep? Explain why.

4 Look at picture **B**. It is connected to the story of Guru Gobind Singh and the first five members of the Khalsa.

   a Find out about the story this picture illustrates.

   b Create a storyboard of the key events of this story.

   c Chose one event from this story to freeze frame.

The Khalsa rules

- Get up early, wash and say the morning prayer
- Recite the evening prayer before going to bed
- Sing the ardas prayer regularly
- Do not take tobacco, drugs or alcohol
- Do not have sex outside of marriage
- Give 10 per cent of your earnings to charity
- Must not eat meat that has been ritually slaughtered
- Wear the **Five Ks**
- Take on the name 'Kaur' if you are a woman and 'Singh' if you are a man
- Treat all Khalsa members as brothers and sisters

OVER TO YOU

Let's reflect

Do you think it is important to have a ceremony to mark when someone joins a community?

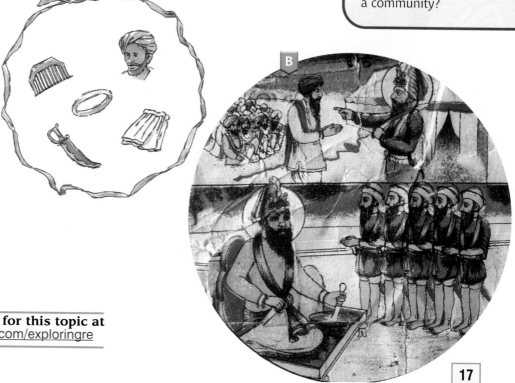

B

WEBLINKS **You will find links for this topic at** www.nelsonthornes.com/exploringre

What can we find out about joining other religious communities?

This is about ...

- **Making personal choices about an area of research**
- **Developing research skills**
- **Learning about different religious communities and some of their beliefs and practices**

In the last three topics you have studied what it means to belong to the Christian and Sikh communities. You are now going to have the opportunity to investigate what it means to belong to another religious **community**. In this section you will ask and answer questions about what religious people do and believe.

Key questions

- **What does it mean to make a commitment to your faith?**

KEY WORDS

- **Beliefs**
- **Commitment**
- **Community**
- **Practices**

OVER TO YOU

Choose one religious community and find out the answers to the following questions. Write up your findings as a short report. Include pictures and diagrams if you can.

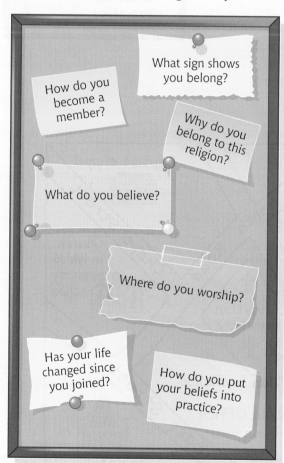

What sign shows you belong?

How do you become a member?

Why do you belong to this religion?

What do you believe?

Where do you worship?

Has your life changed since you joined?

How do you put your beliefs into practice?

Fantastic Facts

In the 2001 UK census, more than two-thirds of the population claimed they belonged to a religion.

WEBLINKS **You will find links for this topic at** www.nelsonthornes.com/exploringre

In our journey through this unit, we have:

- thought about who we are and what influences us
- considered the communities we belong to
- learned about how some people join their religious communities and some of their beliefs and practices
- thought about what commitment to a religious community means

Key questions

- What makes a **community**?
- What is **diversity**?
- Are all religions the same?
- Why is it important for some people to belong to a religious community?

In this unit you have thought about who you are and what influences you. You have also explored religious communities.

OVER TO YOU

1   Look at maps **A** and **B**.

   a   What do you notice about religion in the community in map **A**?

   b   What do you notice about religion in the community in map **B**?

   c   Compare maps **A** and **B**. What similarities and differences can you find?

   d   Make a religious map of your neighbourhood. Decide whether it is more like map **A** or map **B**.

KEY WORDS

- Beliefs
- Commitment
- Community
- Diversity
- Practices

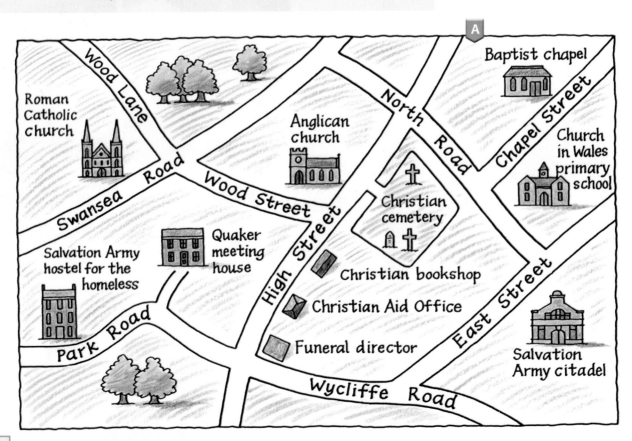

A

Roman Catholic church · Wood Lane · Baptist chapel · Anglican church · North Road · Chapel Street · Church in Wales primary school · Swansea Road · Wood Street · Christian cemetery · High Street · Salvation Army hostel for the homeless · Quaker meeting house · Christian bookshop · Christian Aid Office · East Street · Park Road · Funeral director · Salvation Army citadel · Wycliffe Road

2 As a class, complete a placemat activity about one of the religions you have studied in this unit. Follow these steps:

a Organise yourselves into groups of three or four. Draw an outline of your placemat as shown in the Help! box.

b You will be given a topic. Each member of the group completes an individual section of the placemat template, writing down or drawing all that they know about the topic. Leave the central box blank.

c Each member of the group gives feedback on what they have written to the rest of the group.

d One member of the group acts as a scribe and collates all the relevant information into the central box.

e One member (the scribe) stays with the placemat while the rest of the group move on to the next table.

f The new group, including the scribe, share the information that they have collected on this topic.

g Everyone returns to their original groups and the scribe collates all the additional information into the central box.

h In groups, everyone discusses what they have learnt about their topic.

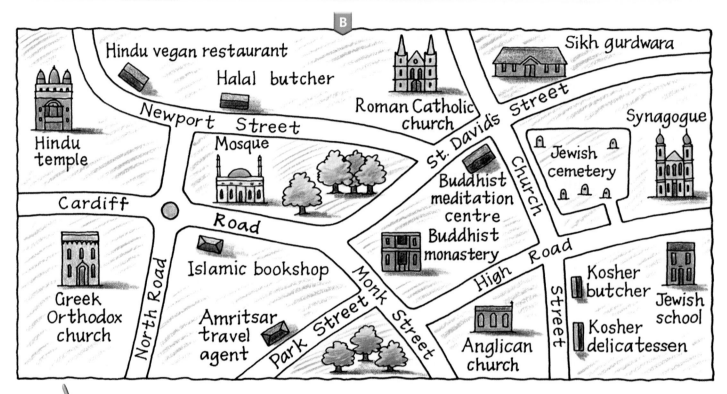

Help!

Placemat activities

Placemat is a group activity where everybody shares what they know about a given topic using a placemat template.

This is about ...

- **Exploring questions about who you are**
- **Considering how you make choices**
- **Making connections between what Christians, Jews, Hindus and Buddhists believe about death and life after death**
- **Understanding how people can show what they believe through words and actions**
- **Evaluating religious beliefs and connecting them with your own beliefs**
- **Asking questions and expressing opinions about issues**

Key questions

- **Who am I?**
- **Am I important?**
- **Why am I here?**

OVER TO YOU

1 What do you want to get out of life? Use the snowball strategy to help you with this question.

Many people ask questions about life and the reasons why we are here. What is the purpose of our existence?

KEY WORDS

- **Beliefs**

Help!

Snowball strategy
This is when a topic is explored by yourself, then in pairs, then in small groups and finally with the whole class.

2 Look at picture **A**. Create your own journey of life map.

  a Include at least three important choices you have made or may have to make in the future as you go through life.

  b Explain your choices to a partner. Who or what has influenced you? For example, did you have a choice of which secondary school to attend? What influenced the final decision?

A

The journey of life

Death is a part of life because the only thing that is certain is that we all will die. When people experience death, whether it is the death of a pet or of someone they know, it often makes them realise that life should be valued. Death can make people focus on what it is that they want from life, and how they can help others.

Some people's lives are cut short by illness. This makes them more determined to live life to the full and to achieve as much as possible. Some even try to help others who may be in a similar situation.

In 2000, doctors told Jane Tomlinson, who is terminally ill with cancer, that she had only months to live. However, she was determined to show that anything is possible. Despite terrible pain, Jane has competed in many marathons such as the Great North Run, the London Marathon and London's Triathlon. She is the first terminally ill competitor to finish all three events and was awarded the Helen Rollason Award at the BBC Sports Personality of the Year Awards in 2002.

Jane and her husband Mike have raised over £400,000 for charity. She believes that while she has time left, she wants to do everything she can to raise money for worthy causes and to achieve as much as possible.

Jane Tomlinson

3 Do you think it is important to help others? How can your life make an impact on the lives of others? Discuss these questions with a partner.

4 As a class, make two lists:
   a Ten things to do before you're 30.
   b Ten things to do before you die.

Fantastic Facts

In 2003, two people around the world died every second. That's more than 172,000 people every day. However, four people were born every second.

Let's reflect

Life begins at 40!

What do you think about the message on this card?

In this unit we will be looking at the way religious people cope with issues of life and death. For many, the choices they make are important. This is because they believe these choices can influence not only their lives now, but also what happens to them when they die.

What happens when I die?

This is about ...

- **Considering different viewpoints about death and the afterlife**
- **Connecting these viewpoints with your own views on death and life after death**
- **Asking questions and expressing opinions**

Key questions

- **What happens when I die?**

KEY WORDS

- Afterlife
- Beliefs
- Death
- Mourner

 Death is Nothing at All

By Henry Scott Holland, who was bishop of St Paul's Cathedral in London

Death is nothing at all. I have only slipped away into the next room. I am I, and you are you. Whatever we were to each other, that we still are.

Call me by my old familiar name, speak to me in the easy way you always used.

Put no difference in your tone, wear no forced air of solemnity or sorrow.

Laugh as we always laughed at little jokes we enjoyed together.

Let my name be ever the household word that it always was, let it be spoken without effect, without the trace of a shadow on it.

Life means all that it ever meant. It is the same as it ever was; there is unbroken continuity.

Why should I be out of mind because I am out of sight?

I am waiting for you, for an interval, somewhere very near, just around the corner.

All is well.

Do Not Stand at My Grave and Weep

Do not stand at my grave and weep

B *I am not there, I do not sleep.*
I am a thousand winds that blow
I am the diamond glints on snow.
I am the sunlight on ripened grain
I am the gentle autumn's rain.
When you awaken in the morning's hush
I am the swift uplifting rush of quiet birds in circled flight.
I am the soft stars that shine at night.
Do not stand at my grave and cry
I am not there, I did not die.

This poem is popular at funerals in the UK

1 Read poems **A** and **B**.

  a What do you think these poems are trying to explain?

  b How do you think their words may comfort someone who has suffered the loss of a special person?

One thing in life is certain – that is we all will die. **Death** is something most people do not like to talk about – it has become a taboo subject.

What happens after death is a 'big' question with no certain answer, but many people have their own views about it. Religious people hold **beliefs** about what happens when you die and we shall explore some of these in the next few sections. However, other people have their own ideas about what happens after death, which are not based on religion:

- Some people believe death is the end of everything, and when you die that is it – the end.

- Some people believe in fate – when your time or number is 'up', that is the end of your life. It is as if your life has already been mapped out for you.

- Some people accept the experience of the feeling of déjà vu. Déjà vu is a general term to explain the feeling you have done, said or felt something before, even though you know you have not had such an experience. Some might interpret this feeling as evidence of being reborn – the belief that life can be lived many times. These strong feelings of déjà vu are seen as memories of parts of a former life.

- Some people believe something happens after death because of a near-death or out-of-body experience. These experiences have been reported by people who have been declared dead by a doctor, only to then come back to life. They report strange things, such as hovering over their own body, moving through a tunnel, seeing a bright light, seeing dead relatives welcoming them and a feeling of happiness and peace. After such an experience, many people feel completely changed by what has happened.

There has been scientific research into near-death experiences and beliefs about past lives. As a result, some people argue that they are caused by the way our brains can be affected by a lack of oxygen, and they are not proof of life after death. Research has neither proved nor disproved that there is life after death. These are matters for personal belief.

However, many people agree that when someone dies their life should be celebrated. In some cultures, **mourners** are asked to wear colourful clothes, play the dead person's favourite music and have a party.

Some people make jokes about death, often to hide their fears

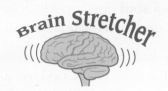

2. Find out what the word 'taboo' means. Use a dictionary to help you and write a definition in your book.

3. Have you ever thought about death? Do you think death is the end? Share your views with a partner.

OVER TO YOU

4. Copy and complete the following sentences.

   a If death were a flower, it would be a _____ because _____.

   b If death were an animal, it would be a _____ because _____.

   c If death were a bird, it would be a _____ because _____.

   d If death were a feeling, it would be _____ because _____.

5. How would you like to be remembered after you have died? Look at the 'In memoriam' column of your local newspaper. Find a verse or saying that appeals to you and copy it into your book.

Brain Stretcher

Does science have all the answers about life and death?

A Caribbean funeral

WEBLINKS You will find links for this topic at www.nelsonthornes.com/exploringre

What do Christians believe about death?

This is about ...

- **Exploring Christian beliefs about death and the afterlife**
- **Understanding how Christians show what they believe through words and actions**
- **Exploring Christian death and burial customs**
- **Asking questions and expressing opinions**

Key questions

- **What happens when I die?**
- **Why should a Christian lead a good life?**

KEY WORDS

- **Afterlife**
- **Beliefs**
- **Cremate**
- **Customs**
- **Denomination**
- **Heaven**
- **Hell**
- **Holy Communion**
- **Hymn**
- **Jesus**
- **Last rites**
- **Mass**
- **Minister**
- **Priest**
- **Resurrection**
- **Sin**
- **Soul**

Christians believe death is not the end of everything but that life goes on after death. They believe this because they believe **Jesus** taught it.

> For God loved the world so much that he gave his only son that whoever believes in him may not be lost but have eternal life (John 3:16).

> I am the Resurrection and the Life. Whoever believes in me will live, even though he dies; and whoever lives and believes in me will never die (John 11:25–26).

The **belief** in the **resurrection** of the dead is important to Christians because they believe Jesus rose from the dead. Jesus's resurrection is seen as a victory over death and **sin**. All Christians believe in an **afterlife**, but not all Christians agree on what this is like. Christians believe everyone has a **soul** or spirit, which does not die when the body dies.

The main belief for all Christians is that, after death, God will judge everyone on how they have lived their lives. Those who have lived according to God's wishes will go to **heaven** to be with God. **Hell** is regarded as not being with God.

1 Read the story of the resurrection of Jesus in the gospel of St John 20–21. Hot seat the reaction of the following disciples to Jesus's resurrection:

a Mary Magdalene (John 20:1–8).

b Thomas (John 20:24–29).

c Simon Peter (John 21:1–19).

Hot seating

This is a drama activity where you imagine what it may be like to be someone else. One student acts as the chosen character and answers questions from the rest of class as though they were that person. Alternatively, the teacher could take the hot seat.

Many Christians believe the Day of Judgement will come, when Jesus will return to Earth, the dead will be raised and their bodies brought back to life. People will be judged on whether or not they can stay with God.

Michelangelo's painting of the Day of Judgement

OVER TO YOU

2 Look at picture **B**. What do you think the artist is trying to show?

3 Create your own piece of artwork to show Christian ideas of heaven and hell.

Christians have some traditional ways of helping people who are dying. Often their **priest** or **minister** visits them to say prayers or to read from the Bible. Some Christians sit and pray with dying people.

In Anglican, Orthodox and Roman Catholic traditions, anointing the sick can take place. When it is performed on a dying person, it is often called the **last rites**. The priest makes the sign of the cross on the person's forehead. If the person is able to receive **Holy Communion** or **Mass**, the priest gives this as well. This is to help them on their final journey. After death, the body may be kept in an open coffin for friends and relatives to say their last goodbye. Sometimes, candles are lit and placed near the body.

The funeral is a time when people say their final goodbye to their loved one. Often, prayers are said, Bible passages read and **hymns** may be sung. The body is either buried in a churchyard or **cremated**. The place of burial is usually marked with a stone or plaque.

A Christian funeral service

4 People sometimes send sympathy cards to friends who have lost a loved one. Write a short verse or phrase that would be suitable for this type of card.

5 Create a fact file that outlines five Christian beliefs about death.

Brain Stretcher

Some people who are not religious wish to have a Christian funeral service. Why do you think they would want to do this?

WEBLINKS **You will find links for this topic at** www.nelsonthornes.com/exploringre

What do Jews believe about death?

This is about ...

- **Exploring Jewish beliefs about death and the afterlife**
- **Understanding how religious Jews show what they believe through words and actions**
- **Exploring death and burial customs in Judaism**
- **Asking questions and expressing opinions**

Key questions

- **What happens when I die?**
- **Why should a Jew lead a good life?**

KEY WORDS

- **Afterlife**
- **Beliefs**
- **Customs**
- **Evil**
- **Festival**
- **Heaven**
- **Hell**
- **Mourning**
- **Rabbi**
- **Rosh Hashanah**
- **Rules**
- **Shroud**
- **Soul**
- **Tallit**
- **Ten Commandments**
- **Torah**
- **Yahrzeit**
- **Yom Kippur**

B

Dear **Rabbi**,
I have to give a presentation to my RE teacher and the rest of my class on 'What Judaism teaches about death and the afterlife'. I would really appreciate your help with this.
Thanks,
James

Dear James,
Belief in an **afterlife** is important to Jews. It goes back to the time of Adam, the first man, when G_d breathed into him the **soul** of life. So we believe the soul is eternal – it never dies. We believe Gehenom, or hell, is part of the world to come. Not all souls go to Gehenom. Gehenom is for people who have done some good but need to be made pure again. Some people are too **evil** for Gehenom and are punished forever. In Judaism, we emphasise living in this world. Only through good deeds in this world does a person earn reward in the next. As Jews, we teach our children that no bad action goes without punishment. At our **festivals** of **Rosh Hashanah** and **Yom Kippur**, we remind ourselves of our actions over the past year. We try to say sorry to G–d and to those who we may have hurt or wronged, asking for their forgiveness. We must do this before all our good and bad deeds are recorded. In order to lead a good life, we follow the **rules** found in our holy book, the **Torah**. These rules help us to live as G–d would want us to live.
The Rabbi

OVER TO YOU

1 Imagine there is going to be a television programme summarising your life.

   a Write down three good things and three bad things you have done in your life.

   b Do you think you have done more good things than bad things?

2 Read the rabbi's reply in box **B**. A rabbi is a Jewish teacher. He said that 'a handful of people are too evil for Gehenom and are punished forever'. Think of five people, from the past or still alive today, who you believe could be considered evil because of their actions.

3 God's rules for people to follow are found in the Torah. Write down five rules that you think would make someone lead a good life.

4 Why is it important for a religious Jew to lead a good life?

Brain Stretcher

Find out more information about the Jewish festivals of Rosh Hashanah and Yom Kippur.

A period of **mourning** takes place after the funeral. Family members mourn for seven days by staying at home and being looked after by friends, who bring them food and encourage them to talk about their loss. After this time, there is a period of less intense mourning when the family returns to work but take no part in any form of entertainment. This lasts for about 30 days after the funeral.

On the anniversary of the death, relatives light a **Yahrzeit** candle, which burns for 25 hours in memory of the person who has died.

Like all religions, Judaism has special **customs** associated with death and burial. Once a person has died, the body is treated with great respect. It is washed and dressed in a linen cloth called a **shroud**, before being placed in a coffin. Jewish men are buried with their **tallit** (prayer shawl) wrapped around their shoulders and with one of the fringes cut. This shows that they no longer have to keep the **Ten Commandments** – laws on how to live as God wishes.

A Yahrzeit candle

OVER TO YOU

5 Imagine you have invited a non-Jewish friend to a funeral. Design a short handout to help them understand what Jews believe about death and mourning customs.

6 Some people say the best way to cope with grief is to get back to everyday life as soon as possible.

   a Do you agree?

   b What might a rabbi say?

7 What advantages and disadvantages can you think of to having a long period of mourning?

8 **a** Do you believe it is necessary to mark the death of a person each year?

   b What would be the benefit of doing this?

What do Hindus believe about death?

This is about ...

- Exploring Hindu beliefs about death and rebirth
- Understanding how Hindus show what they believe through words and actions
- Exploring Hindu death and burial customs
- Asking questions and expressing opinions

A The Hindu cycle of reincarnation

Key questions

- What happens when I die?
- Why should a Hindu lead a good life?

KEY WORDS

- Atman
- Beliefs
- Brahman
- Cremate
- Customs
- Karma
- Moksha
- Mourning
- Rebirth
- Reincarnation
- Symbol

OVER TO YOU

1 Look at picture **A**. What does it tell you about the Hindu belief in rebirth?

Many people believe life does not end with death – there must be something else. Hindus believe in **rebirth**, or **reincarnation**. They believe there is a part of God in all living things. This is called the **atman** (soul). At death, the atman passes on to a new life. This new life depends on how you have lived the present life.

Hindus believe in **karma**. Karma means that everything we do or think affects us in some way. Good actions earn good karma and bad actions earn bad karma. Therefore, if someone is happy, they must have done good things in a past life. If others are suffering, they must have done something bad in a past life.

Hindus believe how you live your present life affects your rebirth. Each rebirth gives the atman the chance to improve and to be reborn into a better life next time around. All living creatures are part of this, so it is possible for people to reborn as animals, insects or plants in their next lives.

Humans are the highest form of life, but the ultimate stage of existence is to break this cycle of birth, life, death and rebirth and achieve release, which is known as **moksha**. This is when the atman is freed from the cycle of reincarnation and returns to its original, pure state. Hindus believe all atmans will eventually be free to join **Brahman**, the one God.

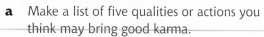

2 Consider the Hindu belief in karma.

   a Make a list of five qualities or actions you think may bring good karma.

   b Make a list of five qualities or actions you think may bring bad karma.

3 Write a short story with two different endings to show how actions can have big effects on those involved. Your story could be based on whether or not to tell a lie to get out of trouble. What happens if you do? What happens if you do not?

4 Design a poster that sums up Hindu **beliefs** about death and rebirth.

Like all religions, Hinduism has special **customs** associated with death and burial. The Hindu belief in reincarnation affects attitudes towards death and how funerals are held.

Hinduism teaches that, although death is sad, especially for those left behind, it is not the end. It is the duty of the family to help the dead person reach their new life. It is important that the heir, usually the eldest son, makes the correct funeral preparations. Once the death has taken place, the funeral is held shortly afterwards. It is desirable for a few drops of water from the River Ganges in India to be placed into the mouth of the deceased. The body is dressed in clean clothes and perfumed with sandalwood.

The body must be **cremated** because Hindus believe fire purifies (cleanses) the body and releases the spirit. The ashes are collected and cast into water because water is believed to be holy. Some rivers, such as the River Ganges, are thought to be very special. It is regarded as a holy river and is a **symbol** of life without end. People come to bathe in its waters and Hindus want to die in the holy city of Varanasi, which is on the banks of the River Ganges. If possible, the ashes are cast into the River Ganges, but any river will do as all rivers lead to the sea, just as all souls eventually join Brahman.

A period of **mourning** then takes place, which is usually between four and thirteen days. According to tradition, the family must first purify themselves by taking a shower and wearing clean clothes. Strict Hindus would have no contact with the outside world during this time. Prayers are said for the person who has died. After the thirteenth day, mourning ends because it is believed that the person has now been reborn.

Hindus do not use memorials like gravestones because they believe the dead person has been reborn. However, they say prayers for their dead relatives on special days.

WEBLINKS **You will find links for this topic at** www.nelsonthornes.com/exploringre

What do Buddhists believe about death?

This is about ...

- **Exploring Buddhist beliefs about death and rebirth**
- **Understanding how Buddhists show what they believe through words and actions**
- **Exploring Buddhist death and burial customs**
- **Asking questions and expressing opinions**

Key questions

- **What happens when I die?**
- **Why should a Buddhist lead a good life?**

Buddhism teaches that death is part of the cycle of life. When one life ends, another life begins. This new life is influenced by how the person has lived their old life.

When the body dies, the energy lives on in another body. It is like the flame of a candle that passes on its energy to light another candle. The ultimate aim of all Buddhists is to end this cycle of **rebirths** and to enter **nirvana**. Nirvana is a state of peace where all selfishness and desire ends. Buddhists believe death is a stepping stone on the road to nirvana.

A

A mandala

KEY WORDS

- **Beliefs**
- **Buddha**
- **Ceremony**
- **Cremate**
- **Crematorium**
- **Customs**
- **Mandala**
- **Meditate**
- **Monk**
- **Nirvana**
- **Rebirth**
- **Shrine**

Buddhists would try to sit with a dying person to **meditate** or read some of the teachings of the **Buddha**. This reminds them of the Buddha's teachings and helps to calm the mind and accept death. Sitting with the dying person in this way is an act of loving kindness. After death, the body is washed and placed in a coffin in the **shrine** room. The funeral takes place either in the shrine room or at a **crematorium**.

Buddhists have some **customs** associated with death and burial that allow friends and family to help the dead person to have a good rebirth. **Monks** chant from holy texts, and family and friends usually donate gifts or food to them. People are encouraged to pass on kind thoughts to the dead person. It is hoped that the goodwill created by these gifts and kind thoughts will help the dead person on their journey. The body is usually **cremated** because the Buddha was cremated. The ashes from the body are either buried in the ground, cast into a river or the sea, or scattered in the wind. However, burial would also be acceptable to Buddhists.

A Buddhist funeral in Narborough, Leicestershire, May 2004

A funeral in Asia

Recall ...

Which other religions prefer to cremate the bodies of the dead?

Remembrance ceremonies are held after seven days, three months and then one a year.

Buddhists believe that life is not permanent but always changing. Nothing lasts forever. They make this point by using sand paintings or **mandalas**. Once made, the mandala is destroyed in a special closing **ceremony**.

Help!

Maps from memory

This is a technique that will help you to use teamwork to make your own copy of a picture. Form small groups. Each person in turn comes to look at the picture for 20 seconds. Do not take any notes. Return to the group and draw from memory for a minute. Then the next student comes up and looks at the picture, memorising for 20 seconds before returning and adding to the picture for a minute. When everyone has had a chance to draw, compare your final drawing with the original picture.

OVER TO YOU

1. How do Buddhists try to help the dead person have a good rebirth?

2. Why is a good rebirth important?

3. Create your own mandala. Base it on photo **A** or research other sources. You could use the maps from memory technique for this activity. Once you've finished it, how would you feel about destroying it?

 **WEBLINKS** **You will find links for this topic at** www.nelsonthornes.com/exploringre

Meaning and purpose in life

In our journey through this unit, we have:

■ made connections between different religious beliefs about death and life after death

■ understood how people can show what they believe through words and actions

■ evaluated religious beliefs and connected them with our own beliefs

■ asked questions and expressed opinions

Key questions

■ **Is it important to remember the dead?**

■ **Do all religions believe the same thing about death and the afterlife?**

KEY WORDS

• **Afterlife**
• **Atman**
• **Beliefs**
• **Cremate**
• **Heaven**
• **Hell**
• **Rebirth**
• **Soul**

In this unit we have explored various viewpoints, both religious and non-religious, about death and **beliefs** in an afterlife. It is important to think about what you believe and whether your study of religion has changed your opinions.

From a young age, many children ask questions about what happens when a person or animal dies. For example:

● what happens when my hamster dies?

● will my rabbit go to heaven when it dies?

● how do we get to heaven – do we grow wings to fly there?

Most people like to remember their loved ones by thinking of the times they have shared with them. They think about their qualities and the experiences they have shared together. Many people like to remember their loved ones by putting flowers on their grave or at home on the anniversary of death. Others put up a memorial. Some famous people have statues, buildings or roads named after them as a memorial. Some examples of these are shown in the photos.

OVER TO YOU

1. Look at photos **A** and **B**, which show memorials to famous people. What other kinds of memorials can you think of?

2. Think of a person you value and respect – someone you know, love or admire. How could you commemorate their life?

A

Dylan Thomas Theatre, Swansea

B

Sir Winston Churchill British prime minister during the Second World War

3 Read the statements in box **C**, which give examples of beliefs held by some religious followers about death and what comes next. Use a large copy of the table below to sort the statements into those believed by Christians, Jews, Hindus or Buddhists. Some statements may apply to more than one faith. The first example has been done for you. Remember to justify your opinions.

Statement	Christian	Jew	Hindu	Buddhist
1			✓	
2				
3				
4				
5				
6				
7				
8				
9				
10				

C

1 There is a part of God in all living things.

2 Those who have led a good life will be rewarded and those who have not will be punished.

3 It is important to sit and spend time with a person who is dying to help them accept death.

4 The body should be **cremated** after death.

5 The body will be reborn in another form.

6 Death will be the end of the physical body and the **soul** or spirit will go to **heaven** to be with God.

7 The funeral must take place as soon as possible after death.

8 **Hell** means separation from God.

9 Death is not the end of everything.

10 Each **rebirth** gives the **atman** the chance to improve and be reborn into a better life next time around.

Book of condolence

We came into this world with nothing, and we shall leave with nothing. But you left behind something, the greatest gift of all – love.

Your memory will live in our hearts forever.

May God's angels watch over you.

God needed an extra angel, that's why he chose you.

May the Lord bless you and keep you. May his light shine upon you and bring you peace.

Your smile, your touch, your love will be greatly missed.

The world is poorer for you not being in it.

D

CONNECTIONS

Find out whether Sikhs or Muslims would accept any of the statements in box **C**.

4 Read the messages in the book of condolence (box **D**). Design a page for a book of condolence from the point of view of one religious tradition. Make up your own messages and add pictures that reflect the beliefs of the religion you have chosen.

5 Imagine you work for a website that gives people answers to tricky questions. Someone has emailed you, asking for help with their RE studies. Choose one faith and explain what members of that religion believe about what happens when we die. Write your response in the form of an email.

6 Copy and complete the following sentences.

  a My idea of heaven is _____.

  b I believe our purpose in life is _____.

  c I believe when we die _____.

  d I think death is _____.

Let's reflect

Can you think of any questions you would like to ask about death and the afterlife? Discuss these with a partner.

3 Religious expression
How do I express myself?

This is about ...

- Considering how people express themselves
- Reflecting on the ways in which religious people express their beliefs and feelings
- Exploring the places of worship for Christians, Muslims and Hindus
- Understanding how actions and rituals help religious people express their beliefs
- Considering how pilgrimage helps people express their beliefs
- Asking questions and expressing opinions

Key questions

- How do people express themselves?
- How can I tell what people are feeling?
- How do people express their **beliefs** and feelings?

KEY WORDS

- **Beliefs**
- **Pilgrimage**

We express ourselves in many different ways. For example, we show our feelings through body language, facial expressions and tone of voice.

OVER TO YOU

1. Look at photos **A–E**. How do you think each person is feeling? Write down your answers, giving reasons for your views.

2. In pairs, discuss and show the body language you could use to show when you are excited, nervous, scared, thoughtful and angry.

Sometimes the clothes people wear say something about themselves or what they do for a living.

OVER TO YOU

3 Look at photos **F–K**. What do the clothes the people are wearing say about each of them?

4 Make a list of your favourite clothes. What do these clothes say about you?

People also use their creative skills to express themselves, such as through poetry, music, art or dance. People who write songs, poems, stories and letters use words to express what they feel about things. Composers express different moods and feelings through their music, dancers do the same when they move their bodies. Painting and drawing are highly expressive too. We also connect with our own feelings when we sing, read poems, watch a performance and look at a piece of art.

Faith CONNECTIONS

Which of these photos **F–K** do you think are connected to a religion? Can you name the religion in each case? Which other faiths use the way believers dress to express beliefs?

OVER TO YOU

5 What is your favourite song? Think about the words – do they have a message? If so, what is it?

6 In pairs, have a short discussion on issues you both feel strongly about. Choose one issue each. Express your feelings about the issue in one of the following ways.

a A design on a T-shirt.

b A song.

c A drawing or painting.

d A poem.

How do Christians express their beliefs? (1) Places of worship

This is about ...

- **Learning about the special features of a Christian church and chapel**
- **Understanding the significance of these key features**
- **Reflecting on the importance of places of worship for Christians**

Many religious people express their **beliefs** by going to **worship** at a special place. Some places where Christians worship include cathedrals, churches, chapels, halls and citadels. The place of worship reflects the kind of worship that takes place there. Christians worship in different ways and these differences are expressed in the design and decoration of their place of worship.

Key questions

- Why do some Christians worship in a special building?

KEY WORDS

- Altar
- Beliefs
- Church
- Cross
- Denomination
- Font
- Jesus
- Lectern
- Minister
- Pulpit
- Rules
- Sermon
- Symbol
- Worship

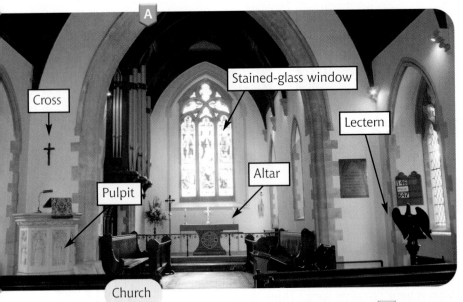

A

Cross
Pulpit
Stained-glass window
Altar
Lectern
Church

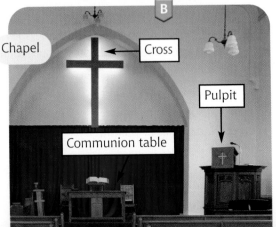

B

Chapel
Cross
Pulpit
Communion table

Recall ...

Have you ever visited a Christian place of worship? If so, what do you remember about the visit?

OVER TO YOU

1 Look at photos **A** and **B**.

  a What differences can you see between the church and the chapel?

  b What features are similar in the two places of worship?

Brain Stretcher

Find out more information about each of the features labelled on photos **A** and **B**. What is their main purpose?

*I worship at St David's Church. It is beautifully ornate. The people who built it wanted to show their love of God by using expensive materials such as gold to decorate the church. The **altar** is always decorated with a beautiful cloth embroidered by members of the congregation. We also have a number of banners. My favourite one says, 'God is love'. The stained-glass windows in my church are spectacular. They show pictures of stories from the Bible and famous saints. All these things remind me of the life and teachings of **Jesus** and help me grow in my faith.*

Phillip

Sarah

*I attend my local chapel on a regular basis. It is plain inside, with little decoration. This helps me focus on the word of God that I hear being taught by the **minister** in his **sermon**. The windows are plain glass and offer no distraction.*

OVER TO YOU

2 a What is the difference between the two places of worship they attend?

b Why do you think Phillip and Sarah prefer different places of worship?

3 Design a banner that could be used in a Christian place of worship. You may like to include Christian **symbols** or biblical teachings.

Christians feel it is important to show respect in a church or chapel because they are in God's house.

OVER TO YOU

4 a In small groups, make a list of **rules** that should be followed when you are in a Christian place of worship in order to show respect.

b Share your ideas with the rest of the class.

CONNECTIONS

Find out about places of worship used by other Christian **denominations**, such as the Salvation Army, the Greek Orthodox Church or the Quakers. What are their main features? How do these features help people to worship?

How do Christians express their beliefs? (2) Ways of worship

This is about ...

- **Understanding how Christians express their beliefs through worship**
- **Reflecting on the importance of worship for Christians**

Key questions

- How does worship help Christians express their **beliefs** and feelings?

KEY WORDS

- Beliefs
- Hymn
- Jesus
- Meditate
- Sermon
- Spiritual
- Worship

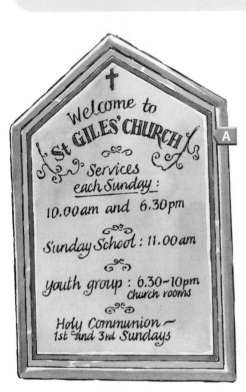

Welcome to **St GILES' CHURCH**

Services each Sunday:

10.00am and 6.30pm

Sunday School: 11.00am

Youth group: 6.30~10pm church rooms

Holy Communion — 1st and 3rd Sundays

A

I try to attend my local church every Sunday. I enjoy worshipping in the church. It's my way of spending time with God and thanking him for everything. It's also important to me to spend time with other Christians. Attending the service on Sundays makes me feel spiritually refreshed, and this helps me through the rest of the week.

Cath

*I'm very busy during the week. Sunday is a special day for me. It's a day of reflection when I pause to think about God and **Jesus**. I find that attending a service in church helps me concentrate on my prayers.*

Steph

During Christian **worship**, the actions and body language of the worshippers helps them express how they feel and what they believe.

OVER TO YOU

1 **a** Look at picture **A**. Make a list of the different activities that could often take place in a church.

b Why do you think Christians involve themselves in such activities?

Let's reflect

OVER TO YOU

Why do you think some religious people benefit from spending time during a busy week to reflect and get in touch with their **spiritual** side?

Christian worship

2 Look at photos **B–E**, which show Christians worshipping. What do the actions say about the feelings and beliefs of the worshippers?

Words play an important part in many different kinds of Christian worship through readings from the Bible, preaching **sermons**, talking about experiences and feelings with others, singing **hymns** and saying prayers. During prayer, a believer speaks to God. One well-known prayer is the prayer of St Francis of Assisi, (box **F**).

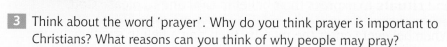

Lord, make me an instrument of your peace
Where there is hatred, let me sow love
Where there is injury, pardon
Where there is doubt, faith
Where there is despair, hope
Where there is darkness, light
Where there is sadness, joy
For your mercy and for your truth's sake
Amen

Peace prayer of St Francis of Assisi

3 Think about the word 'prayer'. Why do you think prayer is important to Christians? What reasons can you think of why people may pray?

4 **a** Read the prayer of St Francis of Assisi in box **F**. How can Christians be 'instruments of [God's] peace'?
b Is the message of the prayer still relevant in the world today?
c Write your own peace prayer.

Music is a form of religious expression. It enables people to make contact with their spiritual side. Many Christians feel that music and singing helps them express their feelings. It also helps them concentrate and remember important ideas about God. **Meditating** (sitting quietly and thinking) is also important to some Christians. It is a way of calming the mind and gaining inner peace.

5 In pairs, discuss the words of any hymns you sing during acts of collective worship at school.
a Can you remember any of the verses?
b What do you think the words mean?

6 Some Christians worship in silence. Have you ever sat silently for a period of time? If so, what did it feel like?

You will find links for this topic at www.nelsonthornes.com/exploringre

How do Hindus express their beliefs?

This is about ...

- Learning about the special features of a Hindu mandir
- Understanding the importance of worship for Hindus
- Understanding how worship helps Hindus express their beliefs
- Reflecting on the importance of worship for religious Hindus

Key questions

- Why do some Hindus worship in a special building?
- How does worship help Hindus express their beliefs and feelings?

1 Look at photos **A** and **B**, which show two Hindu temples. How can you tell they are special buildings?

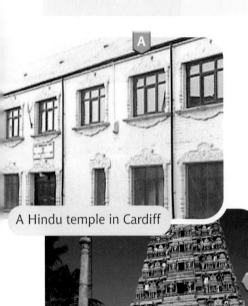

A Hindu temple in Cardiff

A Hindu temple in India

42

KEY WORDS

- Arti
- Arti lamp
- Beliefs
- Ceremony
- Mandir
- Murti
- Prashad
- Ritual
- Worship

Many Hindus **worship** in a **mandir** (temple). The Hindu mandir is considered to be a special place where humans and gods meet. Like many places of worship in the UK, there are different kinds of mandir. For example, they can be purpose-built like the marvellous temple in Neasden, London, or they can be in a building that was used originally for something else. The Hindu temple in Cardiff (photo **A**) was once a nightclub.

Hindus express their feelings and beliefs about God through worship. Hinduism is an ancient religion that has developed over a long period of time. Hindu worship can take many forms. Believers perform actions and **rituals** to express their belief in God and to please God.

When believers enter the mandir, they ring a bell to say they have arrived. Then they take off their shoes and wash their hands. They bring gifts of flowers, fruit or money and these are presented to the **murti** (image of the god or goddess).

One of the most important **ceremonies** in Hinduism is the **arti** ceremony. This is when an **arti lamp** is lit and passed around in a clockwise direction in front of the murtis while a prayer is said. The flame is passed around the believers. They hold their hands above the flame and then raise their hands over their heads. They believe that by doing this they are receiving God's blessing. At the end of the arti ceremony, worshippers are given **Prashad**. This is food offered to and blessed by the Gods and then shared with the worshippers. It can consist of fruit, nuts, sweets or a spicy mix.

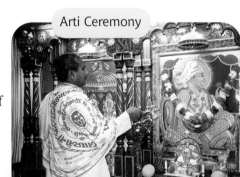

Arti Ceremony

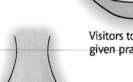

The sound of **God is** described as Aum, the noise that is made when **blowing** into a conch shell

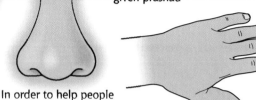

In order to help people focus on God, lamps and incense are burned in the mandir

Visitors to the mandir are given prashad

During the arti ceremony, worshippers move their hands over the holy flame

The murtis can help Hindus to 'see' God

Tejan

Hindu worship appeals to all five senses

2 Imagine you are visiting a Hindu temple during the arti ceremony. Write a poem on Hindu worship that focuses on the five senses – what you see, smell, taste, hear and feel.

3 We have seen that Hindu worship appeals to the five senses. In pairs, discuss the following questions.

  a What item of food would remind you of something important to you?

  b What smell would remind you of something important to you?

  c What sound would remind you of something important to you?

  d What item to touch would remind you of something important to you?

  e What visual object would remind you of something important to you?

Share your ideas with the rest of the class.

4 Like most religious believers, Hindus worship both at home and in the mandir. Why do you think many Hindus feel it is important to worship in a mandir?

5 What would be your ideal place of worship? Which items would help you to worship? Make notes of your ideas and discuss them in small groups.

Even though I worship at home every day, I also visit the temple once a day, usually for the arti ceremony. We sometimes have visitors in the temple for the ceremony – people want to see what happens during Hindu worship. They are sometimes amazed at how noisy worship can be! There is always a lot of singing, clapping and chanting. Musical instruments are also played. Visitors are also surprised that worshippers come and go during the ceremony – many wander in when they are able to come. People also say how colourful the temple is.

OVER TO YOU

Let's reflect

'*He who offers to me with devotion only a leaf, or a flower, or a little water, this I accept from that yearning soul, because with a pure heart it was offered with love.*'

This quote is from a Hindu holy book. Why do you think Hindus usually give something to God in the mandir?

You will find links for this topic at
www.nelsonthornes.com/exploringre

How do Muslims express their beliefs?

This is about ...

- **Learning about the special features of a mosque and their significance**
- **Understanding the importance of prayer for Muslims**
- **Reflecting on the importance of worship for Muslims**

As well as being a place of prayer and **worship**, **mosques** are also places of learning and somewhere to meet. They are designed to reflect the worship that happens in the building.

Key questions

- **Why is the mosque important for Muslims?**
- **Why is prayer important?**
- **What beliefs are Muslims expressing though worship?**
- **How do Muslims express their beliefs through prayer?**

A The outside of a mosque in Cardiff

Dome

C The inside of the Cardiff mosque

Calligraphy

Mihrab

Minbar

Prayer mat

01443 269691

B

Minaret

Prayer hall

A mosque in Dubai

KEY WORDS

- **Allah**
- **Beliefs**
- **Calligraphy**
- **Five Pillars**
- **Hajj**
- **Makkah**
- **Mihrab**
- **Minaret**
- **Minbar**
- **Mosque**
- **Pilgrimage**
- **Qur'an**
- **Rak'ah**
- **Ramadan**
- **Salah**
- **Sawm**
- **Shahadah**
- **Worship**
- **Wudu**
- **Zakah**

OVER TO YOU

1. Look at photos **A–C**. Find out more information about each of the key features labelled. What is their main purpose?

One important aspect of worship in Islam is prayer. Prayer is one of the **Five Pillars**. The Five Pillars are the five main duties Muslims should do. They are called pillars because they hold up the Muslim way of life. The Five Pillars are **Shahadah** (declaration of faith), **Salah** (prayer), **Zakah** (giving to charity), **Sawm** (fasting during **Ramadan**) and **Hajj** (going on **pilgrimage**).

Salah is a special sequence of actions and words to **Allah**. Each sequence of movements is called a **rak'ah**. The worshipper stands, bows, kneels and bows to the ground during a rak'ah. When Muslims pray they stand shoulder to shoulder in rows and face the direction of the holy city of **Makkah**.

Before praying, Muslims must wash in order to make sure they are clean and in the right frame of mind for prayer. This ritual washing is called **wudu** and it involves washing the hands, mouth, nose and face, the arms up to the elbows, the head, ears and feet.

To help Muslims worship, Islamic art is often used. It can be seen in mosques and Muslim homes. One form of Islamic art is called **calligraphy**. Passages written in beautiful calligraphy from the Muslim holy book, the **Qur'an**, are often used as a form of decoration in mosques. Another form of Islamic art is arabesque, which is the combination of geometric and floral patterns. When looking at Islamic art, it is important to remember that pictures of people and animals are forbidden.

D

Calligraphy

E F

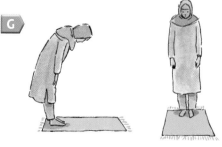
G

H

The sequence of prayer movements called a rak'ah

I

Worship and prayer are important to me. Prayer is a time when I feel close to Allah. Whether I go to the mosque or pray at home, it gives me a sense of peace. Everything I do expresses what I have been taught and what I believe. I wash to purify my body in Allah's presence. When I bow down, I'm showing my willingness to submit myself and show my humbleness to Allah.

Yusuf

OVER TO YOU

2 Look at pictures **E–I**.

  a What do you think the believers are expressing in their prayer movements?

  b Suggest why Muslims pray in rows and stand close together.

  c In which direction do Muslims face when praying? Explain why.

Brain Stretcher

Men and women worship and pray separately in the mosque. Why does this happen? Do you think it is a good idea?

OVER TO YOU

3 Find out why Muslims do not allow people and animals to be shown in their art.

WEBLINKS **You will find links for this topic at** www.nelsonthornes.com/exploringre

Why is Lourdes special to Christians?

This is about ...

- **Understanding the meaning of the term pilgrimage**
- **Understanding why Lourdes is a special place for Christians**
- **Reflecting on how pilgrimage helps Christians express their beliefs**

OVER TO YOU

Key questions

- **Why are some places special to Christians?**
- **Why is Lourdes special to Christians?**

KEY WORDS

- **Beliefs**
- **Pilgrim**
- **Pilgrimage**
- **Sacred**
- **Spiritual**

We all make journeys in our everyday life. We travel to school, visit friends and relatives, go to the shops, watch our favourite football team. Sometimes we make a special journey to a place we have not visited before for a holiday or to go to a special event.

1 Think about some of the journeys you have made in the past year. Make a list of places you have visited and explain the reasons for your visit.

2 Think about one special journey you have made. Where did you go? What preparations did you make? Describe you feelings before, during and after the journey.

People who belong to a religion sometimes go on a special journey to a **sacred** place for a **spiritual** experience. This journey is called a **pilgrimage**. **Pilgrims** usually visit a place because it is linked to a person or an event that is important in their religion.

Journeys take us to all kinds of places

I visited Lourdes last year with a local Catholic organisation. I'm very ill at the moment. Even though I knew it would be a long journey to Lourdes, I'm glad I made the effort. The journey has given me real inspiration and I feel stronger mentally. I feel I now have the strength to fight my illness.

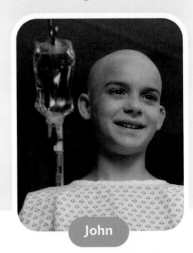

John

Paul

I'm a member of the local Catholic organisation called the Pilgrim's Trust. Every Easter I visit Lourdes in France with this organisation. A group of children and teenagers come with us on the trip. Most of the children are very ill. Each of us is responsible for one child. Before we go, we get to know the children, often meeting for an outing. Last year, I was responsible for a 12-year-old boy called John. I find Lourdes is a very special place. It is a spiritual place. Many of the people at my office ask me why I spend my holidays taking someone to Lourdes. It is difficult to explain, but making the pilgrimage offers me an opportunity to help someone. It makes my faith even stronger.

Pilgrim's Passport

Name: Paul

Religion: Christian

Place visited: Lourdes, France

Why do people visit the place of pilgrimage?
People visit Lourdes because of a famous story associated with this place. It is the story of Bernadette Soubirous. In 1858, Bernadette had a number of visions of the Virgin Mary. Over the years, many people have claimed that they have been healed there.

Preparations for the visit: We have special prayer meetings and also arrange a number of different events to raise money to cover the trip.

What happens during the pilgrimage? We hold a service at a special shrine where people hope to receive healing. Candles are lit to say prayers for people who are ill. People drink the holy water.

Thousands of pilgrims travel to Lourdes each year

Fantastic Facts

At least 65 miracles at Lourdes have been certified as true by the Roman Catholic Church.

WEBLINKS **You will find links for this topic at**
www.nelsonthornes.com/exploringre

OVER TO YOU

3 Imagine you are a volunteer for the Pilgrim's Trust. You need to write a letter to your boss, asking for time off work to take sick children to Lourdes. Describe what you expect to do while you are on the pilgrimage and explain why.

4 Write a postcard from Lourdes to your family and friends back home. Write about what you have been doing and how you feel.

5 Find out about the story of St Bernadette of Lourdes. It was there that Roman Catholics believe the Virgin Mary appeared to her.

Brain Stretcher

Investigate another place of pilgrimage for Christians. Fill in a pilgrim's passport like the one below for a Christian visiting the place.

Name: _____

Religion: _____

Place visited: _____
_____

Why do people visit the place of pilgrimage?
_____
_____

Preparations for the visit:
_____
_____

What happens during the pilgrimage?
_____
_____

Why is Makkah special to Muslims?

This is about ...

- **Understanding why Makkah is a special place for Muslims**

- **Reflecting on the Muslim experience of pilgrimage as a form of religious expression**

Key questions

- Why are some places special to Muslims?

- Why is Makkah special to Muslims?

The most important place of **pilgrimage** for Muslims is **Makkah**. **Hajj** – pilgrimage to Makkah – is one of the **Five Pillars**. All Muslims should try to make the journey to Makkah at least once in their lifetime. **Muhammad**, the most important **prophet** in Islam, was born in Makkah. He also performed a number of religious rituals in the city.

KEY WORDS

- **Five Pillars**
- **Hajj**
- **Ihram**
- **Ka'bah**
- **Makkah**
- **Muhammad**
- **Pilgrimage**
- **Prophet**

OVER TO YOU

1. Look carefully at the pictures of the Hajj. In pairs create some questions that you would like to ask about Hajj using the five Ws template. At the end of your work on the Hajj look again at your questions. Check whether your questions have been answered.

Recall ...

What are the other four Pillars of Islam?

Help!

Five Ws
This is an activity that helps you think of questions starting with the words What, Where, Who, When and Why.

A

B

Some of the things Muslims do on Hajj

C

D

*I went on Hajj to Makkah for the first time last year. It was amazing. There were thousands of Muslims – you really feel you belong to one big family. Most of the men were wearing the **ihram** like me – that made me feel special. There were a number of things to do during Hajj and in some sense it was hard, especially in the heat. The highlight for me was circling the **Ka'bah**. I've seen so many pictures of it before, but it was exciting to be so close to such a special place. It was also special because I knew I was following in the footsteps of our Prophet. I feel so proud to be a Muslim and to have the chance to visit our holy city.*

Pilgrim's Passport

Name: Amin

Religion: Muslim

Place visited: Makkah, Saudi Arabia

Why do people visit the place of pilgrimage? Muhammad was born in Makkah and he lived there for many years.

What do Muslims wear during the Hajj?: Men often wear the ihram – two pieces of white cloth without seams. Women often wear loose, white clothing.

What happens during the pilgrimage?

- Visit the mosque in Makkah. Run and walk anticlockwise around the Ka'bah seven times. Try to kiss or touch the black stone of the Ka'bah.

- Run seven times between the two mountains of As-safa and Al-Marwa

- Spend the night at Mina

- Spend noon until dusk on Mount Arafat

- Throw seven small pebbles at three concrete pillars ('stoning the devil')

- Celebrate the festival of Id-u-Adha.

2 Design a poster to be displayed in the window of a travel agent, advertising a trip to Makkah for Hajj.

3 Imagine you are a Muslim who has just returned to the UK from Hajj. You have been invited to discuss your experiences with members of the local mosque. Describe what happened during your time in Makkah, as well as your feelings before, during and after Hajj. You could use a fortune line graph for this.

a Write the main stages of the Hajj on small cards or Post-it Notes.

b Consider how you may be feeling at each stage.

c Place the cards or Post-it Notes on your fortune line graph.

d Explain your graph to others in the class.

Fortune line graphs

Fortune line graphs help to explain your feelings and emotions as time goes by. The horizontal axis represents time. The vertical axis represents a range of emotions. When you place your cards on the fortune line, you need to think carefully about each event and where it should be placed on the graph.

Time

You will find links for this topic at www.nelsonthornes.com/exploringre

Do all religions have special places?

This is about ...

- **Making personal choices about an area of research**
- **Developing skills of enquiry**
- **Learning about religious pilgrimage**
- **Understanding why places are regarded as special to religious believers**
- **Reflecting on the experiences that people have when on pilgrimage**

Key questions

- **Why are some places regarded as special or sacred?**

KEY WORDS

- Pilgrimage
- Sacred

In the last two sections you have discovered why Lourdes and Makkah are special places for Christians and Muslims. You are now going to have the opportunity to investigate other places of **pilgrimage** and to find out why they are important to members of a particular faith.

After doing a great job on a poster about Hajj, you have been invited by an international tourist board to design a leaflet informing visitors about a place of pilgrimage in their country. Look at a range of leaflets advertising tourist attractions to give you some ideas about how you could structure your leaflet.

How do I create my leaflet?

Identify the religion and place of pilgrimage. The photos on these pages may give you some ideas.

Collect information about:
- the location of the place of pilgrimage
- reasons why people visit this place
- things that happen during the pilgrimage

Information can be found from various sources, such as:
- textbooks
- videos
- interviews with members of the religion
- materials produced by the religion
- websites and CD-ROMs

Present your findings. You could use ICT to create your leaflet. If possible, include:
- a map showing the location
- pictures of the place of pilgrimage
- quotations from people who have visited the place, explaining the purpose of their visit and its effect on them

When you are happy with your finished leaflet, present it to the class

The Golden Temple, Amritsar

The Western Wall, Jerusalem

Bodhgaya, where the Buddha was enlightened

Dome of the Rock mosque, Jerusalem

The River Ganges, India

Walsingham, Norfolk

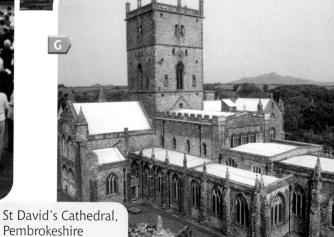

St David's Cathedral, Pembrokeshire

 WEBLINKS **You will find links for this topic at** www.nelsonthornes.com/exploringre

In our journey through this unit, we have:

- recalled what we have learned about religious expression
- reflected on the ways in which religious and non-religious people express their beliefs and feelings
- made connections between how followers of different religions have similar ways of expressing their beliefs
- given our own opinions about religious expression

Key questions

- What does the term 'religious expression' mean?

KEY WORDS

- Beliefs
- Pilgrimage
- Spiritual
- Worship

In this unit we have looked at the many ways people can express themselves through words, actions, clothes and music. We have also looked at how religious people express their **beliefs** by visiting special buildings, performing acts of **worship** and visiting places of **pilgrimage**.

OVER TO YOU

1 Create a mindmap of the various ways that religious people can express their beliefs.

2 **a** Look at photos **A–J**. They show some of the ways people express their religious beliefs. Sort the photos into the following categories to show different types of religious expression.

- Religious worship
- Religious clothing
- Visiting special places
- Work in the community

b Is there anything in the photos that you know has something to do with religious expression but you are unsure what it is? Find out about it.

Help!

Mind maps

Mind maps are a visual way of recording information. Put the key word or main idea into the centre of a sheet of paper. Put all the ideas that come into your head in any order, but draw lines connecting each thought to another like branches on a tree. Take each new idea as far as you can. Use pictures, symbols and words to map out your ideas. Use colours or shapes to highlight important ideas.

In this unit we have looked at why religious people go on pilgrimage to special places. Some of the reasons are as follows.

- To fulfil a religious duty.
- To gain **spiritual** strength.
- To experience God.
- To be healed.
- To meet other people from the same religion.
- To have time to reflect.
- To listen to a religious leader.
- To remember special events in the history of their faith.
- To pray.

3 Read the reasons why religious people go on pilgrimage.

   a Can you add any more reasons to the list?
   b Sort the reasons relating to the places you have studied in this unit, Lourdes and Makkah. Use a large copy of the table below to help you. The first example has been done for you.

Reason	Lourdes	Makkah	Other place of pilgrimage studied
To fulfil a religious duty		✓	
To gain spiritual strength			
To experience God			
To be healed			
To meet other people from the same religion			
To have time to reflect			
To listen to a religious leader			
To remember special events in the history of their faith			
To pray			

4 Create a memory aid on what you have learned in this unit. It could be a:

   a poem..
   b song.
   c quiz.
   d spider diagram.
   e flow chart.
   f grid or table.

4 The existence of God
What is belief?

This is about ...

- **Thinking about and reflecting on your own beliefs**
- **Making connections with religious beliefs**
- **Understanding religious and non-religious views on ultimate questions**
- **Recognising 'religious' questions, which often do not have a definite answer**
- **Asking questions and expressing your own opinions about 'big' questions of meaning**
- **Learning about what some Christians, Hindus and Buddhists believe about God**
- **Exploring the ways believers experience and respond to God**

Key questions

- **What do I believe?**

KEY WORDS

- Beliefs
- Ultimate questions

We all ask questions about the world in which we live because nature is so fantastic. Look at the poem in box **A**, which asks some questions about the world. Some of the questions we may wish to ask about the world are hard to answer, so they are called **ultimate questions**. In this unit we will be exploring **beliefs** that people hold, how these beliefs influence people, and how they can help us find answers to life's ultimate questions.

Religions tackle some of these ultimate questions, such as:

- Is there a God?
- What is God like?
- How did the world begin?
- What happens when we die?

Millions of people around the world follow a religion for the inspiring answers it provides to life's big questions.

A

I wonder

I wonder why the grass is green,
And why the wind is never seen?

Who taught the birds to build a nest,
And told the trees to take a rest?

Or when the moon is not quite round,
Where can the missing bit be found?

Who lights the stars, when they blow out,
And makes the lightning flash about?

Who paints the rainbow in the sky,
And hangs the fluffy clouds so high?

Why is it now, do you suppose,
That Dad won't tell me, if he knows?

from *Come Follow Me* by Jeannie Kirby

Faith is important in all religions. Having faith means believing in something without having any definite proof. It means taking something on trust. Most important things in life depend on trust. For example all money relies on trust. On every bank note it states, 'I promise to pay the bearer on demand the sum of...' This means the bank has promised the holder of the note that, when asked, they will give them the value stated in gold or coins.

Religious beliefs often cannot be proved scientifically, so religious people have faith in their beliefs. This means believers can find answers to the big questions in life that science cannot answer.

Everyone has beliefs and believes things for different reasons. Sometimes we believe something because we have worked it out for ourselves, sometimes because we have evidence or proof, and sometimes we believe things because our culture has taught us or people around us believe it.

OVER TO YOU

1 Copy and complete the three statements of belief found in box **C**.

2 Write three of your own statements of belief.

3 In pairs, discuss some beliefs you feel strongly about. Try to explain why you feel so strongly about them. Did anyone or anything influence the beliefs you hold?

I believe oxygen exists because...

I believe my country deserves to win the football World Cup because...

I believe my best friend cares for me because...

Do beliefs matter?

This is about ...

- **Learning about how beliefs can influence people's lives**
- **Exploring what religious people believe about God**
- **Reflecting on your own beliefs and those of others**

Key questions

- **How do my beliefs affect how I live?**

Some people feel what they believe is so important that they live by those principles. Look at these examples of people who live by their **beliefs**.

Grace

*As a Christian, I believe God expects us to live by his **rules**. One of those rules says that killing is wrong. I am a Quaker and a **pacifist**. Since a very young age, I have been taught that all forms of violence are wrong. My religion teaches me that I should not kill and I take this to mean that I should not harm any living creature. That is why I have been a **vegan** for as long as I can remember. I would never fight in a war or work in the armed forces.*

James

*I believe strongly that we should do everything we possibly can to help the **environment** because otherwise we won't have a world to pass on to our children. I believe God created the world and expects us to act as stewards or caretakers by looking after it. We have a religious duty to do this. I try to help the environment in lots of ways. I recycle everything I can. I sort all my rubbish into boxes containing cans, bottles and papers and take them to collection banks. As a family, we try to eat **organic** food. It can be difficult for my children sometimes because they want to eat the same food as their friends. We feel every small contribution helps our world to continue to be a beautiful place.*

KEY WORDS

- Beliefs
- Community
- Environment
- Organic
- Pacifist
- Ramadan
- Rules
- Sabbath
- Vegan

I help out at a shelter for homeless people. We take food to the shelter and serve it to the residents. Lots of other Muslims come to help at the moment because it's **Ramadan**. *Ramadan is a time for thinking of those who are poor and for giving time to the* **community**. *Most of the people at the homeless shelter aren't Muslim, but we are all a community, aren't we? Since 11 September 2001, Muslims here have tried to show the community what Islam is really all about. It's really important that we do this.*

Hamza

Let's reflect

'Please leave this planet as you wish to find it.'

'The earth has enough for everyone's need but not for everyone's greed.'

Discuss these sayings.

4 Read the quotes in box **A**.

  a Which beliefs are described in each of the quotes?

  b How would these beliefs affect the way someone would live their lives?

1 Read what Grace says.

  a What does the word 'pacifist' mean?

  b What reasons does she give for not showing violence to anyone or anything?

  c What do you think it may be like to be a pacifist in wartime?

2 Read James's statement.

  a Would you like to live in a family like the one described? Explain your answer.

  b Do you believe we should try to protect the environment? Explain why.

  c How could you make a difference to the environment in the way you live your life? Try to include things you do already that are environmentally friendly. Use the snowball strategy to help you with this question.

  d Do you hold any beliefs that are so important to you that they would affect the way you live?

3 Read what Hamza says.

  a Why would other Muslims come to help out at the shelter during Ramadan?

  b Do you think actions are better than words in trying to explain your beliefs to someone who does not share them? Explain your views.

A

Remember to keep the **Sabbath** *as a holy day (Exodus 20:8).*

Guard your eyes and thoughts with rules of modesty in dress (Surah 24:31).

Hear O Israel the Lord our God is one. These words which I command you this day shall be upon your heart. You shall teach them carefully to your children and you shall write them on the doorposts of your house and upon your gates (Deuteronomy 6:4–9).

You must not cook a young goat in its mother's milk (Exodus 23:19).

CONNECTIONS

For which two religions is the command to keep the Sabbath day special an important teaching? What are their holy books called?

Help!

Snowball strategy

This is when a topic is explored individually, then in pairs, then in small groups and finally with the whole class.

What do we mean by ultimate questions?

This is about ...

- **Thinking about and reflecting on your own beliefs**
- **Making connections with religious beliefs**
- **Recognising 'religious' questions, which often do not have a definite answer**
- **Asking questions and expressing your own opinions about ultimate questions**

Key questions

- Why are **ultimate questions** difficult to answer?

KEY WORDS

- Beliefs
- Ultimate questions

In the last section we looked at some **beliefs** people hold and how they influence them. For many people, what they believe helps them make sense of the world in which they live. They feel their beliefs answer those big questions of life – questions that are difficult to answer. This section explores some of these ultimate questions.

What do you think a scientist or doctor may say about some of these questions?

Let's reflect

Life is like a tin of sardines and we're all looking for the key.'

(Alan Bennett, British writer and dramatist)

Look at picture **A**.

1 **a** What do you think about the questions in the diagram? Do any of them have answers? What do you think the answers might be?

  b Do you think everyone in the class agrees with you?

  c How could you persuade someone who does not agree with you that you are right?

2 Think about what you already know about different religions. What might a religious person say about some of these questions? Share your ideas with the rest of the class.

3 Can you add another question of your own? Discuss the answer with a partner and share your ideas with the rest of the class.

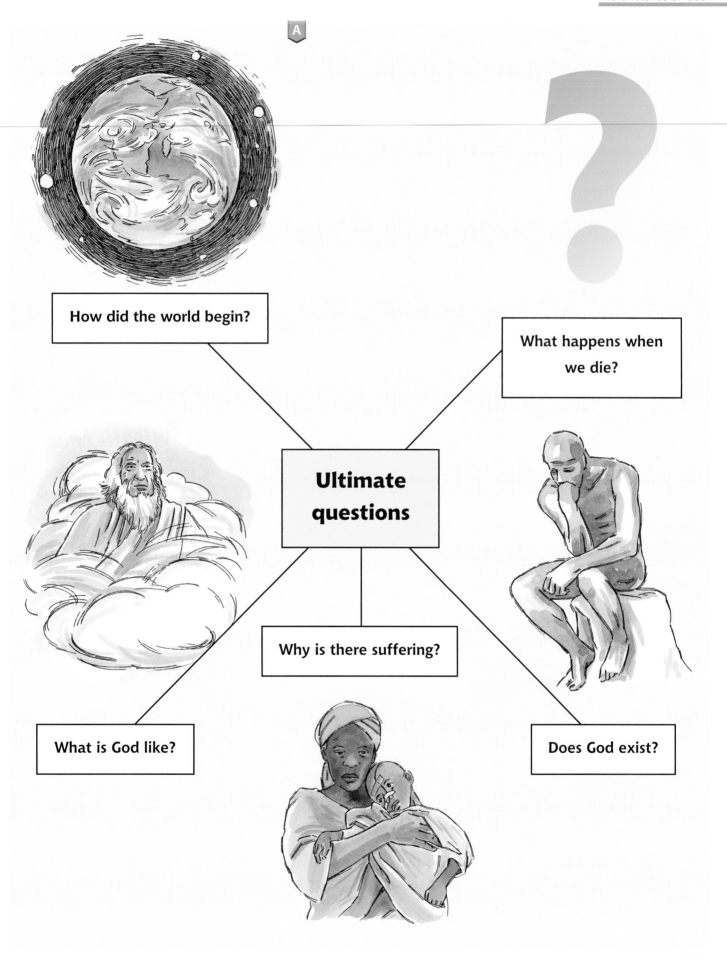

A

How did the world begin?

What happens when we die?

Ultimate questions

What is God like?

Why is there suffering?

Does God exist?

Is there a God? (1)

This is about ...

- **Considering different viewpoints, both religious and non-religious, about the existence of God**
- **Expressing your own views and beliefs about the existence of God**

Key questions

- **Does God exist?**
- **What is God like?**

KEY WORDS

- **Agnostic**
- **Atheist**
- **Beliefs**
- **God**
- **Humanist**
- **Theist**
- **Ultimate questions**

For many people, **ultimate questions** about the meaning of life can only be answered by believing in **God**. Such people are called **theists**. They believe God gives purpose to the universe and meaning to human life. Many theists believe God created and cares for all things and, by following God's will, our existence does not end with death.

However, not all people believe in the existence of God. Some believe there is just the world we live in now and what happens to us is our own doing. They believe we should live for the present and make the most of our opportunities while we are alive, because when we die we will exist no more. Such people are called **atheists**. Atheists are people who believe that God does not exist.

Others say we cannot know whether or not God exists because it cannot be proven one way or another. They are not prepared to say there is no God, but equally they do not say they believe in God. They think big questions such as 'why is there suffering?' or 'why do people die?' are really important but impossible to answer. Such people are called **agnostics**. An agnostic is someone who believes it is not possible to know whether or not there is a God.

Fantastic Facts

If you use Google to search the Internet for the word 'God', you get 115 million results.

OVER TO YOU

1 In pairs or small groups record in a form of a mind map all the things that come to mind when you hear the word 'God'.

Fantastic Facts

In 2004 a research company found out that 75% of people in the UK said that they believed in a god.

Help!

Mind maps

Mind maps are a visual way of recording information. Put the key word or main idea into the centre of a sheet of paper. Put all the ideas that come into your head in any order, but draw lines connecting each thought to another like branches on a tree. Take each new idea as far as you can. Use pictures, symbols and words to map out your ideas. Use colours or shapes to highlight important ideas.

Faith · Faith · Faith

CONNECTIONS

Find out what a **humanist** believes.

Some views of God

A

2 I believe some force was responsible for making the world.

I cannot describe God because he is perfect. **1**

3 What does the word 'God' mean? I don't think there is such a thing.

4 If God exists, why is there so much suffering in the world?

9 I'm not sure if I believe in God. However, I think that if God did exist he would not be a kind, old man with a long beard who lives in the sky.

10 I believe God is like the wind. We cannot see him, but we can feel him. This is how he shows us he is there.

I know God exists because I have personally experienced his power in my life. **12**

11 I don't think the idea of a God makes sense. I think someone made it up just like a fairy story.

5 I believe God is everywhere. We can see him in the beauty of the world around us.

My faith in God is what has given me the strength to face up to life's difficulties.

8

Although I'm not sure whether or not God exists, I think it's good that people have something to believe in.

There is no proof that God exists. **7**

6

2 Read the statements in box **A**. Which statements do you think would be made by a theist, an atheist or an agnostic? Use a large copy of the table below to help you. The first example has been done for you.

Statement	Theist	Atheist	Agnostic
1	✓		
2			
3			
4			
5			
6			
7			
8			
9			
10			
11			
12			

3 In small groups, design a short questionnaire that asks people whether or not they believe in God and their reasons for doing so. Choose ten people, such as members of your family, friends or fellow pupils, to try out your questionnaire. Present your results to the rest of the class.

Let's reflect

'Were there no other evidence at all, the thumb alone would convince me of God's existence.'

(Sir Isaac Newton, British scientist, 1643–1727)

 You will find links for this topic at www.nelsonthornes.com/exploringre

Is there a God? (2)

This is about ...

- **Considering different viewpoints, both religious and non-religious, about the existence of God**
- **Expressing your own views and beliefs about the existence of God**

Key questions

- **Does God exist?**
- **What is God like?**
- **Is there good and evil in the world?**

KEY WORDS

- **Atheist**
- **Awe**
- **Beliefs**
- **Evil**
- **Sacred**
- **Theist**

People who believe in God (**theists**) say it is possible to learn about God in a variety of ways. They say that just by looking at the world around us we can see evidence that God exists. This evidence can be found in the beauty and design of nature.

OVER TO YOU

1 What things in nature would fill many people with **awe** and wonder?

Some theists would also say that many things in the natural world seem to be so well suited to their purpose. Things could not have worked out so well by accident – someone must have designed them. For example, consider the camel with its humps for storing water during long journeys across the desert. Could that have happened by chance?

There is also the evidence from people who have experienced God themselves – through prayer, visions, a voice inside them and many other ways. People of faith have done amazing, wonderful things through history and in the world today, and their experiences of God working through them is an inspiration to many believers. For many religious people, **sacred** texts provide a rich and powerful record of God's messages to mankind.

However, there are also things that happen in the world that are cruel and cause much suffering. Humans themselves often do evil things. This leads to other questions, such as:

- If God is good, why would he design a world where bad things could happen?
- If God can do anything and knows everything, why would he allow such things to happen?
- If there was no evil or suffering, would people know what was good?
- If God made all people good, would we not be his robots?

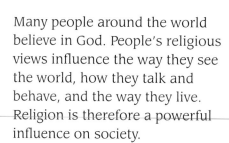

2 Look at photos **A–I**, then answer the following questions. Explain your answers in each case.

  a Which of these pictures could a theist use to suggest that God exists?

  b Which of these pictures could an **atheist** use as evidence that God does not exist?

  c Think of an argument for each picture from both sides.

Many people around the world believe in God. People's religious views influence the way they see the world, how they talk and behave, and the way they live. Religion is therefore a powerful influence on society.

In 2001, the UK Census collected information about religious identity. Box **J** shows which religion people said they belonged to.

UK population by religion

Religion	Number of people	Percentage of population
Christian	41,014,811	71.8
Muslim	1,588,890	2.8
Hindu	558,342	1.0
Sikh	336,179	0.6
Jewish	267,373	0.5
Buddhist	149,157	0.3
Other	159,167	0.3
No religion	8,596,488	15.1
Not stated	4,433,520	7.8
All population	57,103,927	100.0

J

Fantastic Facts

Although the religious Census question was voluntary, over 92 per cent of people chose to answer it.

3 Look at box **J**.

  a Does anything about this information surprise you?

  b What percentage of the population said they were Christians?

  c After Christianity, what was the next most popular faith?

Brain Stretcher

What changes in the numbers of believers and non-believers would you predict for the 2011 Census?

WEBLINKS **You will find links for this topic at** www.nelsonthornes.com/exploringre

How do Christians see God?

This is about ...

- Learning about what Christians believe about God
- Understanding why beliefs are important for religious people

Key questions

- Why do Christians believe in God?
- What is God like?

A

I believe in God, the Father almighty,
creator of heaven and earth.

I believe in **Jesus** Christ, his only Son, our Lord.
He was conceived by the power of the **Holy Spirit**
and born of the **Virgin Mary**.

He suffered under Pontius Pilate,
was crucified, died, and was buried.

He descended to the dead.
On the third day he rose again.
He ascended into heaven,
and is seated at the right hand of the Father.
He will come again to judge the living and
the dead.

I believe in the Holy Spirit,
the holy catholic Church,
the communion of saints,
the forgiveness of **sins**,
the **resurrection** of the body,
and the life everlasting.

Amen

The Apostles' Creed, a statement of Christian belief

KEY WORDS

- Beliefs
- Creed
- Holy Spirit
- Jesus
- Resurrection
- Sin
- Trinity
- Virgin Mary

CONNECTIONS

The word 'catholic' means 'universal', so in the Apostles' **Creed** it applies to both Roman Catholics and Protestants.

OVER TO YOU

1 Read the Apostles' Creed in box **A**. What key Christian **beliefs** does it express?

Most Christians would make the following statements of belief:

 B

> I believe there is one God who is all-powerful. God can do anything.

> I believe God knows everything about us and the world in which we live.

> I believe God is everywhere. He is all around us.

> I believe God created the world.

> I believe God is eternal. God was never born and will never die.

> I believe God will judge the world.

> I believe God is one but there are three parts to him. God can be known or experienced through God the Father, Jesus his son and the Holy Spirit. This is called the **Trinity**. All three are parts of the one, just like a shamrock has three leaves that are all part of the same plant.

> I believe Jesus was God's son, who was born of the Virgin Mary. Jesus was both human and God. I believe Jesus died to save the world.

2 Read the statements of belief in box **B**.

a Think of two more Christian beliefs and write them in speech bubbles in your book.

b Design a poster showing some of the key Christian statements of belief. Explain your choice of images.

3 a On a small piece of paper, write down one question you would like to ask God.

b Put the questions from the whole class into a box. Each pupil should then take a question from the box.

c In small groups, imagine you are having a conversation with God. Ask your questions and discuss what you think God's responses would be.

I couldn't imagine living without believing that God is always with me. I contact God through prayer. It's like calling your friends on the phone to have a chat. I talk to God in this way but I also listen to what God tells me.

Caroline

You will find links for this topic at
www.nelsonthornes.com/exploringre

How do Hindus see God?

This is about ...

- **Learning about what Hindus believe about God**
- **Understanding why beliefs are important for religious people**

Key questions

- **Why do Hindus believe in God?**
- **What is God like?**

Hinduism is one of the world's oldest religions. It teaches that there is one God, but that God can appear in many different forms. Most Hindus believe God is both one and many, rather like someone with different qualities. Think of yourself – although you are one person, you are different things to different people.

1 **a** Draw a spider diagram of people who know you, such as friends, parents, brothers and sisters.

b Underneath each person, write how you think they may describe you.

c Are all the descriptions the same?

Spider diagrams

This is when a main idea (the body of the spider) is explored further (spider legs).

Some of the main **beliefs** of Hinduism are as follows.

- There is one God (**Brahman**), who is also known by other names like **Brahma**, **Vishnu** and **Shiva**. These three together are called the **Trimurti**.

- God reveals himself through **avatars**, which he sends to Earth in human form. **Rama** is one such avatar.

- God is everywhere and in all things.

- God is eternal and never dies.

- God is neither male nor female.

- God is **spiritual** so we cannot see or hear him.

- Each soul (**atman**) is a tiny part of God.

When Hindus greet one another, they bow and put their hands together as a sign of respect to the atman within each other. Hindus usually worship God through one or two of the many thousands of different **deities** (gods and goddesses, including avatars) that are part of God. Believers have statues or images (**murtis**) of the gods in the **mandir** and at home. These murtis help people focus on God.

KEY WORDS

- **Atman**
- **Avatar**
- **Beliefs**
- **Brahma**
- **Brahman**
- **Deity**
- **Durga**
- **Ganesha**
- **Hanuman**
- **Krishna**
- **Mandir**
- **Murti**
- **Rama**
- **Shiva**
- **Spiritual**
- **Trimurti**
- **Vishnu**

Hindus often press their hands together when they greet each other

Rishma

As a Hindu, I try to think about God every day – it's very important to me. I need to feel close to God. I can do this at home or in the mandir by worshipping our special image of God called a murti. Our family god is Vishnu, the preserver. He has four arms.
We show our love for Vishnu by bringing him gifts of food and flowers. I think about Vishnu a lot. I try to remember stories about him. If I feel frightened or worried about anything, I pray to Vishnu and it helps my bad thoughts go away. I feel peace in my mind.

OVER TO YOU

2 This is a research task on Hindu murtis. Use the jigsaw activity for this task.

   a Your teacher will give you the name of a Hindu murti to research in expert groups.

   b After you have returned to your home groups, design a poster presenting all you have learned about each murti. Include pictures and drawings if you can.

A

Brahma, Vishnu and Shiva together make up the Trimurti

Help!

Jigsaw activity
This is a strategy that uses both home and expert groups. The class is divided into four or five small groups called 'home groups'. Each member is given the name of a topic to research and become an expert in. Everyone then joins their corresponding experts from the other groups, forming 'expert groups'. They research the same topic using the resources provided. Everyone returns to their home groups and shares the information they have collected.

B

Hanuman

Krishna

Durga

Ganesha

Some popular Hindu gods and goddesses

OVER TO YOU

Let's reflect

God is One, but wise men call Him by different names.'
(Rig Veda 1.164.46)

 **WEBLINKS** **You will find links for this topic at** www.nelsonthornes.com/exploringre

What do Buddhists believe in?

This is about ...

- **Learning about what Buddhists believe**
- **Making connections between what different religions believe about God**
- **Understanding why beliefs are important**

Key questions

- **What do Buddhists believe in?**
- **Why is the Buddha important to Buddhists?**

KEY WORDS

- **Anatta**
- **Anicca**
- **Beliefs**
- **Buddha**
- **Dharma**
- **Dukkha**
- **Enlightened**
- **Meditate**
- **Nirvana**
- **Rebirth**
- **Ultimate questions**

Buddhists do not believe in a God. They do not believe in a great creator of the world that we see in other faiths. In most religions, people follow a way of life that leads to God, but Buddhists follow a way of life that leads to **nirvana**. This is not an actual place but a state of peace where all selfishness ends. It is beyond the cycle of birth, death and **rebirth**.

Buddhists follow the teachings of the Buddha, who lived in India about 2,500 years ago. His name was Siddhartha Gautama. He was given the title of 'Buddha', which means 'the **enlightened** one'. Buddhists honour the memory of the Buddha because they believe he was a special, wise and holy person. Buddhists do not believe the Buddha was God but an enlightened human being. They see him as a great teacher. He is a role model for them and how they should live their lives.

A

The Buddha's life

Siddhartha Gautama was born a prince in India. At birth, the wise men said he would become either a great king or a holy man. His father wanted him to become a great king and made sure he did not see anything to take him away from his royal duties. He was kept within the palace walls. Siddhartha married and had a son. One day, he wandered outside the palace and saw four sights. The four sights were an old man, a sick man, a dead man and a holy man. From this, he understood that all people age, suffer and die, but that there was a way to overcome suffering. The face of the holy man showed him this.

Siddhartha could not forget the suffering he had seen and vowed to find out how to bring an end to suffering. He left the palace and his royal life, dressed himself in rags and studied under several teachers. He still could not find the answers he was looking for. He sat down to **meditate**. He was tempted to stray from his path of seeking understanding, but he did not give in. By overcoming temptation, he understood the truth in life and became enlightened. He set out to teach others what he had learned. He died at the age of 80.

Although Buddhists do not believe in God, they do have **beliefs** that help them answer some of life's big questions. The teachings of the Buddha are called the **dharma**. Some of these teachings include:

- the belief in **anicca** – life is always changing and nothing is permanent, including the self. Some of the most beautiful things, such as flowers, have a short life. Even humans are always changing and are not here permanently. We will all die.

- the belief in **anatta** – there is no soul and no self that lives on when we die. The Buddha taught that when we die the energy lives on and is reborn in another body. It is like the flame of a candle. The flame can be used to light another candle. The candle itself is not passed on, just the flame.

- the belief in **dukkha** (suffering) – the failure of ordinary life to give complete satisfaction. The Buddha taught that suffering can be stopped by not craving and wanting things. The right way is shown by following the guidelines called the Eightfold Path. These guidelines advise people not to harm others and to train the mind to overcome all desires.

1 Create a fact file by choosing key facts about the following events in the Buddha's life. Use the events as headings in your fact file.

   a Birth.
   b Childhood.
   c Early adulthood.
   d The search for truth.
   e Enlightenment.
   f Teachings.
   g Death.

Golden Buddha

Let's reflect

Lord of the Rings star Orlando Bloom has become a Buddhist. Do you know of any other celebrity Buddhists? What do you think Buddhism has to offer them?

2 **a** Write down three things you really want in life.
   b In pairs, discuss your lists and explain your choices.
   c Ask your partner to think of reasons why fulfilling the things on your list may not give you lasting happiness. Do the same for your partner's choices.
   d Do you know anyone famous who appears to 'have it all' but is still unhappy? Explain your choices.
   e What could non-Buddhists learn from the Buddha's teaching that craving causes suffering?

3 What do you think a Buddhist might say in answer to these **ultimate questions**:

   a Is there a God?
   b Why is there suffering?
   c What happens when we die?

WEBLINKS **You will find links for this topic at** www.nelsonthornes.com/exploringre

Can people come to know God?

This is about ...

- **Understanding why belief in God is important to religious believers**
- **Exploring the ways believers experience and respond to God**

Key questions

- **Does God exist?**
- **Can people come to know God?**

Theists say it is possible to learn about God in a variety of ways. Beauty and wonder in the world around us give us evidence that God exists. They also claim that God can make himself known to people in a more personal way. Some people feel they have met God or have heard stories of others who have met him. Sometimes people say they have had visions or other extraordinary experiences of God.

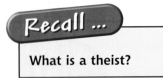

Recall ...

What is a theist?

However, most believers would probably say they have come to know God in fairly ordinary ways. Perhaps they have read passages from their holy books, heard a **sermon** or spoken to someone else who believes in God. Many people say God has spoken to them or they have had some real experience of God while they were praying, reading or **worshipping**. Others have heard an 'inner voice' speaking to them while they were doing ordinary things.

Here are some examples of ways believers have experienced God.

A

Shane Lynch

Shane Lynch, the former singer with Irish boy band Boyzone, has also transformed from a hard-drinking 'Mr Angry' to a committed Christian. Anger, violence and drink problems saw him hit rock bottom before a chance encounter with a Christian friend made him think about God and religion. Soon after, Shane experienced a **conversion**. He worked hard to turn his life around and put his career back on track. He says he owes everything to **Jesus** and now feels his life is a brand-new adventure that gets better every day.

KEY WORDS

- **Atheist**
- **Beliefs**
- **Conversion**
- **Jesus**
- **Sacred**
- **Sermon**
- **Theist**
- **Worship**

Nia

The Welsh singer Nia became a Christian at the age of 10. She is passionate about sharing the love she found in her Christian faith with others. Nia felt God was calling her to share her gifts with those less fortunate in the world. She set up Nia International Activities and uses the profits from the sale of albums and merchandise to sponsor her mission trips. As Honorary Vice President of The Samaritan's Purse, formerly known as Operation Christmas Child, she has visited many countries to demonstrate in practical ways the 'love in action' philosophy.

People experience God through worship

God can also be experienced through reading the **sacred** texts

OVER TO YOU

1 a How would an **atheist** view these religious experiences?
  b How could they explain them?

2 Do you think a conversion experience would change the way someone lives their life? If so, how do you think they may change?

3 Find out about the work of Samaritan's Purse. Design a poster to advertise this organisation and to encourage people to donate to their cause.

Brain Stretcher

What arguments might a theist use to convince an atheist that God exists?

I can recall the day I became a Christian. I went to the local Apostolic Church with some mates. The minister asked for people to repent and accept the Lord Jesus Christ. I felt drawn to go to the front. I could hear a voice inside me saying: 'Well, what are you here for? I have work for you to do. Go to the front and become my disciple.' I found myself walking to the front of the church. When the minister put his hands on my head, I felt a warm glow and God speaking to me again, saying: 'I love you and you are now one of my sons.' God still speaks to me through this voice within.

Aidan

CONNECTIONS

Find out about some of the following people and the experiences that changed their lives:
● The Apostle, Paul.
● Muhammad.
● Martin Luther King.
● Muhammad Ali.
● Nicky Cruz.
● Yusuf Islam (Cat Stevens).
● Bernadette Soubirous.

WEBLINKS **You will find links for this topic at**
www.nelsonthornes.com/exploringre

In our journey through this unit, we have:

- reflected on the importance of belief in God for religious believers

- made connections between different religious beliefs about God

- evaluated these beliefs and compared them with our own

- expressed our own opinions and beliefs about God

Key questions

- **Is there a God?**

- **Do beliefs matter?**

- **Can someone change their beliefs?**

KEY WORDS

- **Beliefs**
- **Jesus**
- **Spiritual**

In this unit we have explored different ideas about belief or non-belief in God.

1. Read the statements in box **A**, which give examples of beliefs about God held by some religions. Use a large copy of the table below to sort the statements into those believed by Christians, Hindus or Buddhists. Some statements may apply to more than one faith. The first example has been done for you.

Statement	Christian	Hindu	Buddhist
1	✓		
2			
3			
4			
5			
6			
7			
8			
9			
10			

1. God can be known through **Jesus**.

2. God is the creator of the world.

3. There is only one God.

4. There is nothing about us that will last forever. There is no soul.

5. God is everywhere.

6. God has the power to do anything.

7. Everything in life changes. Nothing is permanent.

8. God is eternal. He has no beginning and no end.

9. Death is not the end of everything.

10. God is **spiritual** and therefore we cannot see him.

I think God is kind. He lives in the sky and he always knows what we're doing. I think he has a kind face with a long white beard and sits on a big throne. When he is sad he cries, and Mum told me this is why we have rain.

(Sophie, aged 7)

B

2 Read Sophie's thoughts about God in box **B**.

a What ideas of God does she have?

b Have your ideas about God changed as you have grown up? Explain your answer.

c Have your ideas about God changed since you have studied this unit? Explain your answer.

Where is God for you in this picture?

C

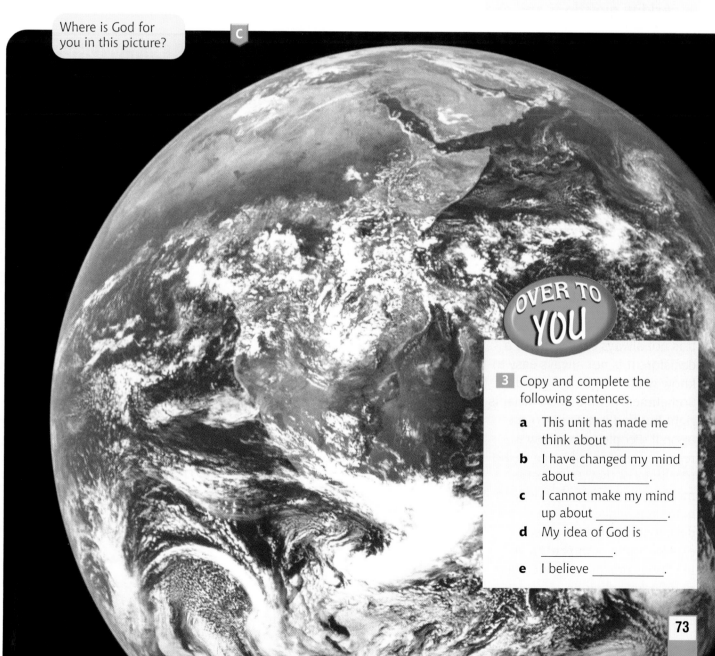

3 Copy and complete the following sentences.

a This unit has made me think about _____.

b I have changed my mind about _____.

c I cannot make my mind up about _____.

d My idea of God is _____.

e I believe _____.

This is about ...

- **Considering decisions and dilemmas that you are faced with and the things that help you to decide what to do**
- **Reflecting on the importance of rules**
- **Learning about religious communities and their rules for living**
- **Reflecting on the connection between rules and behaviour**
- **Asking questions and expressing opinions**

Key questions

- **What decisions will I have to make in the future?**
- **What factors can influence my decisions?**

Every day we are faced with problems and dilemmas to solve. We have to make decisions all the time, sometimes very important ones. Deciding what to do when faced with a dilemma means thinking through these questions:

- What am I going to do in this situation?
- How am I going to behave?
- What would be the right thing to do?

It is not always easy to make a decision. It is not always easy to know what is right and good. Sometimes, people know what is right but find it difficult to act upon it. People who follow a religion turn for guidance to the teachings of their faith or the messages in their holy books to help them make the right decision. In this unit we will explore some of the **rules** and teachings practised by members of different religions.

OVER TO YOU

1. Think about some of the decisions you have had to make recently. Discuss them with a partner. How did you decide what to do? What helped you to decide?

2. In pairs, think about a character in a soap opera you both watch. Identify some of the decisions your character has had to make.
   a. What did they do?
   b. How did they decide what to do?
   c. Do you think they made the right decisions? Explain your answer.

3. In pairs, list some of the decisions most teenagers need to make as they grow up, such as which GCSEs to study, whether to smoke or drink alcohol, where to go on holiday. Share your ideas with the rest of the class.

KEY WORDS

- **Community**
- **Rules**

Help!

Zoom lens board

A zoom lens board is five concentric circles on a large piece of paper. The central circle represents 'Most important', the second circle 'Very important', the third circle 'Important', the fourth circle 'Fairly important' and the fifth circle 'Least important'.

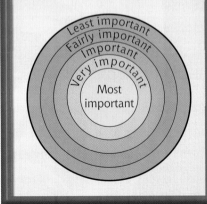

What factors help you make decisions?

Religious teachings?

Local religious leader?

Television?

Magazines?

Teachers?

Internet?

Past experience?

Parents?

Friends?

Conscience?

OVER TO YOU

4 Look at picture **A**.

a In pairs, discuss how each factor affects your decisions.

b What other factors could influence your decisions?

c You are going to use the zoom lens board strategy for this activity. Write each factor on a small card or piece of paper. Discuss how important each factor is when you need to make a decision. Place each card in the appropriate place on a large copy of the zoom lens board. Explain your answers.

5 Read the letters in box **B**. Consider the dilemmas facing the pupils who wrote the letters. In pairs, choose one letter and write a response. Give the best advice you can to help solve their dilemma.

B

Dear Tom,

I feel very upset at the moment. Some older pupils are bullying me at school. It's making my life a misery. They call me names and steal my lunch. What can I do? Please help.

Dear Tom,

My friend has started to steal things from the local shops. He keeps giving me sweets and magazines, which I know he's stolen. I'm afraid we'll get into real trouble for this. What should I do?

Dear Tom,

When I first started at my secondary school, I felt very lonely. In order to make friends with people, I started telling a few lies about myself. I wanted to impress everyone. This has now got out of hand and I'm worried in case people find out I've been lying. What should I do?

Why have rules?

This is about ...

- **Considering the types of rules in everyday life**
- **Exploring and reflecting on the importance of rules**

We know that during our lives decisions need to be made and they may not always be easy. Certain factors can influence our decisions. Sometimes, rules offer us guidance on what to do and how to behave in certain situations. They can provide us with a framework to help us make the right choices.

Key questions

- **Why do rules exist?**

KEY WORDS

- **Rules**

OVER TO YOU

1. Look at pictures **A–C**. In small groups, discuss the following questions.

   a. Which rules are important in your everyday life?
   b. What are the benefits of following rules?
   c. What are the disadvantages of following rules?

A

C

* Wear slippers not shoes in the house
* No jumping on the beds
* Put the toilet seat down after using it
* Keep your bedroom tidy
* Don't leave toys on the floor
* Make your bed in the morning

B

2 Look at pictures **D–G**. In small groups, discuss the following questions.

a What rules have been broken?

b What happens when we break the rules?

3 Look at box **H**. In small groups, discuss the following questions.

a Devise five rules that you think will be necessary for all housemates to follow. Give reasons for your choices.

b What would be the consequences of breaking any of these rules?

c Share your ideas with others in your class.

d As a class, write a list of rules for everyone living in the house.

Congratulations!

You and nine other teenagers from around the UK have been chosen to take part in a new television reality show. You will all live in a house monitored by cameras 24 hours a day. There will be no adults to supervise you.

Let's reflect

'*A world without rules is a world in chaos.*'

Do you agree? Give examples to support your answer.

What is right and wrong?

This is about ...

- **Considering the meaning of right and wrong, good and evil**
- **Learning about religious ideas regarding good and evil**
- **Exploring and reflecting on good and evil in the world today**
- **Reflecting on your own attitudes to what is right and wrong**

Key questions

- **What is good in the world today?**
- **What is evil in the world today?**

KEY WORDS

- Allah
- Evil
- Free will
- Satan
- Shaytan
- Sin

How do we know which are the right things to do and say, and which are the wrong things? Most of the time, it is something inside us that tells us the difference. This is called our conscience, and it gives us a sense of right and wrong. From an early age, people around us – especially our parents and teachers – also influence us.

OVER TO YOU

1 Look at photos **A–F**.

  a Which pictures would you consider to show 'right' behaviour?

  b Which pictures would you consider to show 'wrong' behaviour?

2 Use the snowball strategy to list any further examples of right and wrong behaviour.

Brain Stretcher

In pairs, discuss how your parents and teachers can influence your ideas of right and wrong.

Help!

Snowball strategy
This is when a topic is explored individually, then in pairs, then in small groups and finally with the whole class.

Michael

I've been in this school for two months now. Since I've been here, I've seen a pupil in my class, called David, being bullied by a group of older pupils. I've seen them being very cruel to him – they take his lunch money and throw his school books in the mud. Last week I even saw them thumping him quite hard and calling him names. This morning, a policeman came to speak to our class. David has run away from home and hasn't been seen for the last three days. The policeman asked us if anyone knew anything about where David was or if he had any problems. I just don't know what to do.

When we read newspapers and watch television, we are aware that humans are capable of great cruelty and that **evil** exists in the world. We are also reminded sometimes that people perform great acts of kindness and do much good in the world. Good and evil are important religious ideas. All the major religions try to explain the struggle between good and evil.

Fantastic Facts

A recent Gallup poll found that 68% of people believe that there is a devil.

Christianity and Judaism teach that God has given human beings **free will**. This means they can live their lives and behave as they choose. Human beings have been given the choice whether to accept or reject God and whether to do good or evil. For many Christians and Jews, evil occurs when people choose to reject God.

Most Christians believe the first humans, Adam and Eve, disobeyed God and introduced **sin** into the world. Since then, people are born with a tendency towards evil. Many believe this evil comes from a supernatural force called **Satan**. Satan appears in the Bible as the enemy of God.

Islam teaches that the source of evil is **Shaytan**, who is the enemy of **Allah**. Shaytan tries to tempt people away from Allah and cause them to do wrong. Muslims believe evil will always be punished. People who cause evil must ask Allah for forgiveness. Allah will always forgive those who are truly sorry for what they have done.

WEBLINKS **You will find links for this topic at** www.nelsonthornes.com/exploringre

OVER TO YOU

3 Read what Michael says.

   a In small groups, consider what options are open to him. Discuss these with the rest of the class.

   b Make a class list of all his options. Allocate one option to each group in the class.

   c In your groups, consider the advantages and disadvantages of the option you have been given.

   d Discuss your ideas with the rest of the class.

   e After listening to the feedback, decide which option would work best if you were in Michael's situation.

4 **a** Create a collage of examples of good and evil in the world today. Use newspapers, magazine articles and information from the Internet.

   b Present your work to the rest of the class, explaining your choices of pictures and articles.

OVER TO YOU

Let's reflect

'Doing what's right isn't always easy, but it's always right.'

Do you agree with this statement?

How should Christians live their lives?

This is about ...

- **Exploring the factors that help Christians decide how to live their lives**
- **Learning about the Ten Commandments and the teachings of Jesus**
- **Reflecting on the relevance and importance of such rules for society today**

Key questions

- **Which factors help Christians make difficult decisions?**
- **Why are the Ten Commandments important to Christians?**
- **What is the significance of the Ten Commandments today?**

For many people, their religion gives them guidance on how they should live their lives. Certain factors can help Christians to make decisions.

Ben

*As a Christian, it is important for me to read the **Bible**. The Bible offers guidance on how I should live my life. I try to read part of the Bible every day. When I have something on my mind, certain passages make things clearer for me. I think about the words and actions of **Jesus** and this helps me understand my situation better.*

OVER TO YOU

1 Read what Charlotte and Ben say.

   a Make a list of the factors that help Christians make difficult decisions.

   b Which factors do you think would help them most? Explain your answer.

The Ten Commandments are an important set of principles for both Christians and Jews. These laws identify how they should behave towards God and towards other people.

Charlotte

*When I have a problem, I often turn to my faith to help me decide what I do. I go to church to pray. It gives me comfort to turn to God for advice and I feel a sense of peace come over me. I also discuss my problems with my Christian 'family' at the church. They have sometimes experienced similar situations. My local **minister** is also supportive and willing to listen.*

KEY WORDS

- Bible
- Jesus
- Minister
- Rules
- Ten Commandments

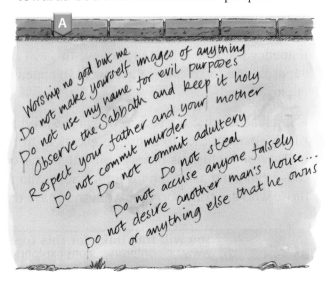

A

Worship no god but me
Do not make yourself images of anything
Do not use my name for evil purposes
Observe the Sabbath and keep it holy
Respect your father and your mother
Do not commit murder
Do not commit adultery
Do not steal
Do not accuse anyone falsely
Do not desire another man's house...
or anything else that he owns

2 Read the Ten Commandments in picture **A**.

a As a class, discuss the commandments and find out the meanings of any words you do not understand.

b Which commandment would be the hardest to keep? Explain why.

c Which commandment would be the easiest to keep? Explain why.

d Which commandment do you think is the most important? Explain why.

e What would the world be like if everybody kept these commandments?

f What would the world be like if nobody kept these commandments?

g Although the Ten Commandments are thousands of years old, many people say they are still relevant today. Do you agree? Are there any issues in today's world that the commandments do not deal with?

In 2004, the Methodist Church and Ship of Fools website asked people to suggest a new commandment to be added to the existing ten. The five winning commandments are shown in picture **B**.

3 Look at picture **B**.

a In pairs, discuss what you think the eleventh commandment could be.

b Write your commandment on a Post-it Note and make a classroom display of all the suggestions.

c As a class, discuss which commandment is the most popular. Can you think of a reason why?

The Bible contains many of Jesus's sayings, which help Christians live their lives as they believe Jesus would have wanted them to do.

4 a Look at the following teachings of Jesus: (John 15:12–13), (Matthew 5:39–40), (Matthew 7:1), (Matthew 6:19–21) and (Matthew 22:36–39).

b Chose the quote that you think is most relevant in society today. Write a short story, draw a picture or role play the scene in order to explain its meaning.

c Jesus taught that you should, 'Love your neighbour as you love yourself'? Think about society today. Do all people treat others as their 'neighbours'?

Jesus lived at a time when Jews were unhappy about the society in which they lived. They were under Roman rule, paying high taxes, being treated unfairly in every way and being punished harshly for any law-breaking. Jesus spoke out against these problems and praised those who were doing good.

5 Think about your own community.

a What things do you think need changing?

b What things would you like to praise and encourage?

c What actions could you take to get your views across to the community?

Why do Jews keep food laws?

This is about ...

- **Considering the factors that help religious Jews decide how to live their lives**
- **Learning about the importance of Jewish food rules**
- **Exploring and reflecting on the practical implications of Jewish rules**

Key questions

- **Which factors would help Jews make difficult decisions?**
- **Why are food rules important for religious Jews?**
- **Why are rules important in the Jewish religious community?**

*I find the **Ten Commandments** helpful when I have to decide what is right and wrong. I'm reminded about them every time I visit the **synagogue** as they can be found above the Holy Ark inside. **Moses** received these Ten Commandments from God on two tablets of stone. They have always been a guide to Jewish people about what is right and wrong.*

Adam

KEY WORDS

- Kosher
- Moses
- Rabbi
- Rules
- Synagogue
- Ten Commandments
- Torah

Rebecca

Sarah

OVER TO YOU

1 Read what Adam, Rebecca, Sarah and Hannah say.

   a Make a list of the factors that help these people make difficult decisions.

   b Can you think of any other factors that may help?

*I get a lot of support from my friends and family when faced with a problem. I also get support from members of my Jewish community, especially at the synagogue. The **rabbi** is always helpful and ready to discuss a number of issues with me. He helps me understand God's teaching.*

*When I have a decision to make, I try to remember what is written in our holy book, the **Torah**. It contains 613 laws.*

Prayer is very important to me because it's my time to talk with God. During prayer, things often become clearer in my mind and this helps me make important decisions.

Hannah

Recall ...

Can you remember what the Ten Commandments are? Why does Christianity have the same Ten Commandments as Judaism?

Fantastic Facts

McDonalds operates both kosher and non-kosher restaurants in Israel

Many Jews follow food rules that tell them what they can and cannot eat. Food that is allowed is called **kosher**. Jews believe God gave Moses these food laws. These rules can be found in Leviticus 11:1–23 in the Torah, and elsewhere in the holy book. For example, based on the teachings of Exodus 23:19, Jews must not cook a young goat in its mother's milk. Therefore, Jews who follow kosher rules do not eat meat and dairy foods together.

A

Kosher rules

Meat – only animals that chew the cud and have cloven hoofs may be eaten.

Sea creatures – only fish that have fins and scales may be eaten. Shellfish are not kosher.

Birds – no birds of prey may be eaten but domestic fowl are allowed.

Meat and milk should not be eaten at the same time. Meat and milk products must be kept separate. Separate pots and utensils are to be used.

Fruits, eggs, vegetables and grains can be eaten with meat or milk products.

Keeping kosher rules can be difficult in countries and communities that are not Jewish. Many foods and non-food products include ingredients that are not kosher. Animal fats are used in a wide range of items, not just foods. For example, vitamin pills and other medicines can include non-kosher ingredients, as can candles, soaps, washing-up liquids and washing powders, sweets, glue, and even plastics. Jews have to take care when purchasing products and read labels carefully to make sure they do not break kosher rules.

We can ask the question therefore, why do many Jews follow these rules?

Some people have shown that they are a good basis for a healthy diet. But for most Jews who keep kosher, the reason is that they believe God wishes it. Judaism teaches that God has given people rules to help them tell right from wrong, good from bad. Keeping kosher in the food they eat is part of trying to follow God's rules in life.

OVER TO YOU

2 Read Leviticus 11:1–23 and look at picture **A**.

a Which foods are considered kosher?

b Which foods are unfit to eat?

c Can you explain why these foods are allowed/not allowed?

Brain Stretcher

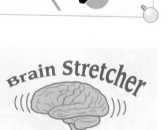

Think about some of your favourite foods. Are they kosher?
How easy would it be for you to keep kosher rules?

Let's reflect

OVER TO YOU

'Keeping kosher isn't hard at all. What makes it difficult is that the rest of the world doesn't keep kosher.'

Would it be a good idea for everyone to follow kosher rules? What are the advantages and disadvantages of doing so?

Kosher food stamp

WEBLINKS **You will find links for this topic at** www.nelsonthornes.com/exploringre

Why do Jews keep Shabbat?

This is about ...

- Considering the factors that help religious Jews decide how to live their lives
- Learning about the importance of Shabbat
- Exploring and reflecting on the practical implications of Jewish rules

Key questions

- Why is **Shabbat** important for religious Jews?
- Why are **rules** important in the Jewish religious **community**?

KEY WORDS

- Community
- Holy
- Rabbi
- Rules
- Sabbath
- Shabbat
- Special
- Torah

Observe the **Sabbath** and keep it **holy**. You have six days in which to do your work, but the seventh day is a day of rest dedicated to me. On that day no one is to work – neither you, your children, your slaves, your animals, nor the foreigners who live in your country. In the six days I, the Lord, made the earth, the sky, the sea, and everything in them, but on the seventh day I rested. That is why I, the Lord, blessed the Sabbath and made it holy.

(Exodus 20:8–11)

A

Shabbat starts at sunset on Friday evening and lasts until nightfall on Saturday evening. These photos show how some Jewish families celebrate Shabbat.

OVER TO YOU

Can you explain what is happening in each of these pictures?

Shabbat is a holy and **special** day. It has been important for religious Jews throughout their long history. Many Jewish families look forward to Shabbat each week as it is such a special occasion.

The **Torah** tells Jews that Shabbat is a day of rest: a day for prayer and family. Shabbat celebrates the freedom Jews have to rest from their everyday stresses and worries and devote themselves to the most important things in life.

There are some things that Jews are not allowed to do on Shabbat. There are many rules in the Torah that forbid 'creative' acts, like making food, lighting fires or lights, and making clothes. This is because God rested from creating things on the seventh day.

In today's world, these rules mean some Jewish families prepare for Shabbat by:

- switching on any lights they will need until Shabbat is over, or putting them on timer switches
- taking the light bulb out of the fridge so it does not light up when the door is opened
- unplugging the telephone
- cooking all food in advance.

For some Jews, keeping Shabbat means:

- not driving a car
- not buying or selling anything not watching television, playing video games or using the Internet.

Some people would say Shabbat is all about restrictions – what you cannot do. However, many Jews would say these laws are what makes Shabbat special. They claim the laws do not stop you doing things – in fact they help you do what is important in life.

Ask the Rabbi

➤ Can I switch on electricity during Shabbat?

➤ Can I warm food during Shabbat?

➤ Can I ask my parents to drive me to a friend's house on Shabbat?

➤ Can I do my homework during Shabbat?

➤ Can I play football with my friends during Shabbat?

➤ What should I do if an emergency happens during Shabbat, such as needing to go to hospital?

➤ I'm Jewish, but I don't see the point in all these Shabbat laws. Why should I bother?

Brain Stretcher

'We need laws in order to be free.'

Do you agree?

2 Read the questions in box **H**.

   a Imagine you are the **rabbi**. How would you answer each of these questions?

   b In small groups, write another question you would like to ask the rabbi.

   c Exchange your question with another group. Answer their question from the rabbi's perspective.

   d Share your questions and answers with the rest of the class.

WEBLINKS **You will find links for this topic at** www.nelsonthornes.com/exploringre

Why do Muslims have rules about food?

This is about ...

- Considering the factors that help Muslims make decisions about how to live their lives
- Learning how Muslims recognise the importance of right and wrong
- Exploring and reflecting on the practical implications of Muslim rules

Key questions

- Which factors help Muslims make difficult decisions?
- Why do Muslims feel it is important to follow their religious rules?
- Which dilemmas could Muslims face if they live in Britain?

The word 'Islam' means 'submission' and a Muslim is someone who submits to the will of God. When faced with a dilemma or difficult decision, Muslims think about what **Allah** expects of them. Muslims try to please Allah in the way they live their lives. They believe Allah knows everything and can see everything. He knows all the answers.

Muslims make no distinction between everyday life and religious life. In order to know how to live their life, they look for guidance in their holy book, the **Qur'an**. Muslims believe the Qur'an is Allah's own words, recited to the **Prophet Muhammad** over a period of many years.

Muslims also have records of the Prophet Muhammad's words and actions as guidance. The **sunnah** is a collection of what the Prophet said and did during his years of teaching, and the **Hadith** is a collection of his sayings. Muslims look to these for help when making decisions.

They can also turn to the **Shari'ah** for guidance. Over the centuries, scholars wrote down Muslim laws for people and communities trying to follow the right path in life. The Shari'ah gives guidance to Muslims on what is **fard**, **halal** and **haram**.

- Something that is fard is a duty and must be done.
- Something that is halal is allowed.
- Something that is haram is forbidden.

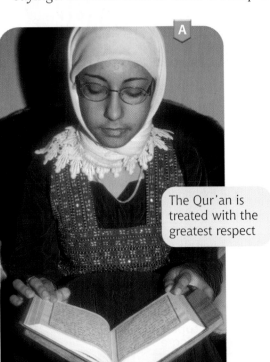

The Qur'an is treated with the greatest respect

KEY WORDS

- **Allah**
- **Fard**
- **Five Pillars**
- **Hadith**
- **Halal**
- **Haram**
- **Muhammad**
- **Prophet**
- **Qur'an**
- **Ramadan**
- **Rules**
- **Shari'ah**
- **Sunnah**

OVER TO YOU

1 **a** What factors help Muslims to make difficult decisions?

b Can you think of any other factors that may help?

2 Think of the rules at your school.

a What things are absolutely forbidden?

b What things must be done?

c What things are allowed, perhaps under certain conditions?

Muslims must eat only food that is halal. This is food that is permitted according to Muslim law. All fish and vegetables are halal. Food that is not fit to be eaten is haram. Any food substance from a pig is haram (because pigs are thought to be unclean), and so is meat from animals that have died naturally. Animals that live by killing others are also haram.

Muslims are allowed to eat meat of other animals if they have been killed according to Muslim law. The throat of the animal must be cut quickly with a sharp knife. Muslims believe this is the most painless way of killing animals. All the blood must be drained out of the animal before the meat is eaten. The person killing the animal must say the name of God. This is to show that a life is being taken with God's permission for a good reason – food.

B

Lawful to you are all things good and pure. Eat of the things that Allah has provided for you, lawful and good.

(Surah 5:4)

C

Does it matter how your food is produced?

Recall ...

What similarities can you see between Jewish food rules and Muslim food rules?

Fasting means going without food and drink. It is called saum and is one of the **Five Pillars** of Islam. It is fard (a duty) for Muslims. Muslims are expected to fast during the ninth month of the Muslim calendar, called **Ramadan**. Muslims go without food and drink from sunrise until sunset. Children under the age of 12 do not have to take part, but many young children are encouraged to fast for a few days. Those who are old, pregnant, unwell or making a difficult journey are also excused.

Lots of my non-Muslim friends say fasting must be really hard. They can't see the point of going without things when you don't have to. Some people have even said to me that it's wrong to fast for religious reasons when so many people in the world have to go without food and water because they're poor.

But for me it is really important for lots of reasons. For a start, it means I know what it's like to be hungry and thirsty. I have a much better idea of what life is like for the really poor people of the world. I think that means I have a lot of sympathy for them and want to help them all I can. My religion is about following the will of God. Fasting makes me resist temptation in order to obey God, and knowing that all my fellow Muslims are going through it too really helps. Then you have a nice meal every night, and at the end of Ramadan there's a fantastic celebration.

Fatima

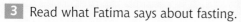

OVER TO YOU

3 Read what Fatima says about fasting.

   a What reasons does she give for fasting?

   b If she was really thirsty and drank a sip of water, and no one saw, do you think that would be OK? Explain your answer.

4 Have you ever tried going without little treats to save up for something you really want? Write down your experiences or make up a story where this happens.

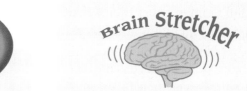

Brain Stretcher

'Fasting is more difficult in a non-Muslim country or community.'

What do you think? Explain your views.

87

Why do Muslims have rules about clothes?

This is about ...

- Considering the factors that help Muslims make decisions about how to live their lives
- Learning about why dress rules are important for Muslims
- Exploring and reflecting on the practical implications of Muslim rules

Key questions

- Why do Muslims feel it is important to follow their religious **rules**?
- Which dilemmas could Muslims face if they live in Britain?

KEY WORDS

- Hijab
- Rules

One thing many people in the UK know about Islam is that there are rules about what women and teenage girls should wear.

Fashionable clothes in western countries are often designed to make people look attractive to others. Islam teaches that men and women should dress modestly. This means Muslim women should not show off their bodies and should not dress in clothes that are revealing. In a few countries, such as Saudi Arabia, local custom means Muslim women cover themselves completely, including their faces. In other countries, such as Pakistan, it is not necessary for women to cover their faces as long as they cover their arms, legs and sometimes their hair.

*I'm a Muslim living in Bangor. When I was younger, I was envious of my friends who were able to wear fantastic clothes. However, as I've got older, I've become more interested in Islam. I see the sense in dressing modestly. I wear clothes that cover up my arms and legs, and I wear a **hijab**. Why do I dress modestly? Well, partly because it's traditional in my culture and because it's a rule in Islam. But I also think it's right for me. I have more respect for myself and expect respect from others.*

Shareen

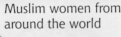
Muslim women from around the world

OVER TO YOU

1. Consider the dress code for Muslims. Write a list of three items of clothing most Muslim women may choose not to wear.

2. Read what Shareen says about dressing modestly. Why has she made this choice?

In June 2004, Shabina Begum, a 15-year-old from Luton, lost a High Court battle for the right to wear a Muslim gown at her school in Luton. Her appeal in March 2005 was successful.

3 Read the newspaper report in box **C**. Why do you think Shabina Begum was not allowed to wear her Muslim gown in school? What arguments may she have made in court, and what arguments might the school have made against her?

Muslim pupil loses legal battle to wear jilbab

A 15-year-old Muslim girl yesterday lost her high court battle for the right to wear strict Islamic dress to school.

From Sam Jones *The Guardian* Wednesday June 18th 2004

Shabina Begum has not attended Denbigh high school in Luton since September 2002 when she was sent home for turning up in a jilbab – the full-length gown worn by many Muslim women that covers all of the body except the face and hands.

Shabina's claim that she had been "constructively excluded" from her school was dismissed by Mr Justice Bennett. He said the school's refusal to let her wear the jilbab did not breach her right to education and freedom of religion as laid down in the European convention on human rights.

The school, a 1000-pupil comprehensive where almost 80% of pupils are Muslim, said it had a flexible uniform policy to ensure that the religious and cultural sensitivities of its students were respected. Girls have the option of wearing trousers, skirts, or a shalwar kameez (trousers and a tunic).

4 Imagine you have been invited to take part in a radio phone-in programme. You are going to discuss some of the problems that Muslim schoolchildren might face living in Britain.

a The class will be divided into six groups, numbered 1–6. Groups 1–3 choose one of the following topics: food, dress or fasting. Each group selects one pupil as the expert on the chosen topic. Group members help the expert by researching their topic.

b Groups 4–6 should come up with a list of questions on the same topics to ask the expert during the phone-in.

c When ready, groups 4–6 should ask the appropriate expert to answer their questions.

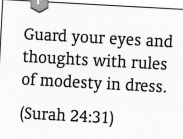

Guard your eyes and thoughts with rules of modesty in dress.

(Surah 24:31)

Let's reflect

It is sometimes difficult being different from others. What difficulties might Muslim teenagers face living in Britain today?

WEBLINKS **You will find links for this topic at** www.nelsonthornes.com/exploringre

How do Buddhists live their lives?

This is about ...

- **Considering the factors that help Buddhists make decisions on how to live their lives**
- **Learning about Buddhist precepts**
- **Exploring and reflecting on the Buddhist precepts**

Key questions

- **Why do Buddhists aim to keep the precepts?**

KEY WORDS

- **Buddha**
- **Karma**
- **Monks**
- **Nuns**
- **Precepts**
- **Rules**
- **Spiritual**

Buddhism does not have a set of **rules** that must be followed by everyone. Instead, they have a number of guidelines. These guidelines are called **precepts**, and they are based on the teachings of the **Buddha**. Buddhists aim to follow these guidelines. The precepts help people avoid actions that may lead to harmful results. They help a person make progress on the **spiritual** path.

A

The five precepts

- ❖ Avoid harming any living thing.
- ❖ Avoid taking what is not given.
- ❖ Avoid harmful sexual activity.
- ❖ Avoid saying what is not true.
- ❖ Avoid alcohol or drugs that cloud the mind.

Buddhist **monks** and **nuns** are expected to follow an additional five precepts. They promise:

- not to eat at inappropriate times
- not to sing, dance or act
- not to use garlands, ornaments and perfume
- not to sleep in a high or broad bed
- not to handle gold and silver.

1 Consider the five precepts in box **A** and discuss the following questions.

   a What is the meaning of each precept?
   b How would each precept affect your life if you were a Buddhist?
   c Would you find the five precepts easy to follow? Explain your views.
   d Which precept would be the easiest to follow? Give reasons.
   e Which precept would be the most difficult to follow? Give reasons.

2 In small groups, write down five rules that would help you to live a good life. Share your ideas with another group. How different are they from the five precepts?

3 Consider the additional precepts that monks and nuns follow.

   a What is the meaning of each precept?
   b Why do you think monks and nuns have more rules to follow?

Buddhists believe in **karma**. This means every action people take has an effect on their circumstances in this life and their future lives.

CONNECTIONS

Which other religions believe in karma?

OVER TO YOU

4 Look at photos **B–D**. Which precepts are being broken?

OVER TO YOU

5 Look at photos **E–F**. Which precepts are being followed?

6 In small groups, choose one of the following scenarios.

THE ORANGE TREE
Vegetarian Restaurant and Take Away

Scenario A

You are at a party at a friend's house. Some of your friends have started to smoke and drink alcohol. They offer you cigarettes and a drink. At first, everyone is friendly and laughs when you say 'no'. Suddenly, the atmosphere changes and your friends put more pressure on you to smoke a cigarette and drink alcohol.

Scenario B

All your friends have a mobile phone and they text each other during the evenings and weekends. You feel left out because you don't have a mobile. One day, you find a mobile in the changing rooms. You are with a friend who tries to tempt you to take it.

a Discuss the scenario and how you think a Buddhist might respond.

b Choose a person in your group to be a Buddhist. Role play the scenario and include what the Buddhist response would be.

WEBLINKS **You will find links for this topic at** www.nelsonthornes.com/exploringre

In our journey through this unit, we have:

- recalled what we have learned about religious and non-religious rules
- reflected on the importance of rules for society
- made connections between religious beliefs and behaviour
- expressed our own opinions about the importance of rules for living

Key questions

- **Why are rules important?**
- **Why are religious rules important for believers?**

In this unit we have studied **rules**, **commandments** and **precepts** that are relevant to Christians, Muslims, Jews and Buddhists.

OVER TO YOU

1. Look at picture **A**. Think about all the different factors that help people decide what to do when faced with a difficult decision. Present the information in the form of a spider diagram. Include things that are important to people of different religions.

2. Think about the rules followed by Christians, Muslims, Jews and Buddhists.

   a. Which rules apply to more than one religion?

   b. Why do some rules apply to more than one faith?

   c. Select one rule which you think is the most important rule. Explain your answer.

3. Which qualities do religious rules try to encourage? Use the snowball strategy to discuss this question. Here are some words to help you.

Helpful   Loving   Honest

KEY WORDS

- **Beliefs**
- **Commandments**
- **Precepts**
- **Rules**

Spider diagrams

This is when a main idea (the body of the spider) is explored further (spider legs).

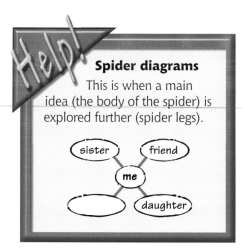

Snowball strategy

This is when a topic is explored individually, then in pairs, then in small groups and finally with the whole class.

B

honesty

Cover your body

helpful

Do not steal

modesty

Love thy neighbour / Help others

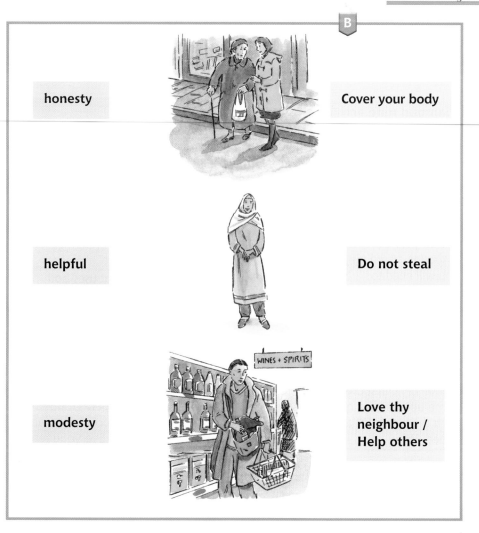

C

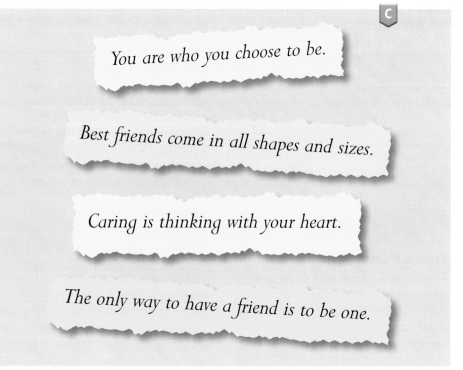

You are who you choose to be.

Best friends come in all shapes and sizes.

Caring is thinking with your heart.

The only way to have a friend is to be one.

Words of wisdom to help people live their lives

4 a Look at box **B**. The words and pictures outline the rules and qualities encouraged by various religions. Can you match each quality and rule to the correct picture?

b Create your own set of triads.

5 Look at box **C**. As a class, design a poster displaying words of wisdom to offer guidance and help in dealing with everyday problems.

WEBLINKS **You will find links for this topic at** www.nelsonthornes.com/exploringre

Diamond nine activities

This is an activity where a list of things is rearranged in order of priority. The most important thing is placed at position 1. Continue to prioritise each item in the list until the least important is placed at position 9. You can do this on your own or in groups. In groups you will need to discuss your choices to reach a joint decision.

Five Ws

This is an activity that helps you think of five key questions. For any topic, come up with five questions starting with the words What, Where, Who, When, Why.

Fortune line graphs

Fortune line graphs help to explain your feelings and emotions as time goes by. The horizontal axis represents time. The vertical axis represents a range of emotions. When you place your cards on the fortune line, you need to think carefully about each event and where it should be placed on the graph.

Freeze frame

This involves setting up a scene as if it were a video freeze frame or a still from a movie. You need to choose a scene from the story and freeze it. You need to be able to describe how each character in the freeze frame is thinking and feeling at that precise moment.

Hot seating

This is a drama activity where you imagine what it may be like to be someone else. One student acts as the chosen character and answers questions from the rest of class as though they were that person. Alternatively, the teacher could take the hot seat.

Jigsaw activity

This is a strategy that uses both home and expert groups. The class is divided into four or five small groups called 'home groups'. Each member is given the name of a topic to research and become an expert in. Everyone then joins their corresponding experts from the other groups, forming 'expert groups'. They research the same topic using the resources provided. Everyone returns to their home groups and shares the information they have collected.

Maps from memory

This is a technique that will help you to use teamwork to make your own copy of a picture. In small groups, take it in turns to look at the picture for 20 seconds. Do not take any notes. Return to the group and draw from memory for a minute. Then the next student comes up and looks at the picture, memorising for 20 seconds before returning and adding to the picture for a minute. When everyone has had a chance to draw, compare your final drawing with the original picture.

Mind map

Mind maps are a visual way of recording information. Put the key word or main idea into the centre of a sheet of paper. Put all the ideas that come into your head in any order, but draw lines connecting each thought to another like branches on a tree. Take each new idea as far as you can. Use pictures, symbols and words to map out your ideas. Use colours or shapes to highlight important ideas.

Placemat activities

Placemat is a group activity where everybody shares what they know about a given topic using a placemat template.

Snowball strategy

This is when a topic is explored individually, then in pairs, then in small groups and finally with the whole class.

Spider diagrams

This is when a main idea (the body of the spider) is explored further (spider legs).

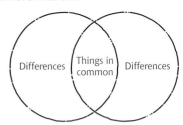

Venn diagrams

Venn diagrams show what things have in common, and what the differences are.

Zoom lens board

A zoom lens board is five concentric circles on a large piece of paper. The central circle represents 'Most important', the second circle 'Very important', the third circle 'Important', the fourth circle 'Fairly important' and the fifth circle 'Least important'.

Keywords

A

Afterlife – a belief that there is life after death

Agnostic – someone who believes it is not possible to know whether there is a god or not

Allah – the Muslim name for God

Amrit – a Sikh holy drink made of sugar and water that has been blessed

Anatta – a Buddhist belief that there is no such thing as a permanent soul or self

Anicca – a Buddhist belief that everything changes and nothing or no-one stays the same

Arti – a welcoming ceremony when offerings are made to a Hindu god

Arti lamp – a lamp used during the Arti ceremony.

Atheist – someone who does not believe that God exists

Atman – Hindu belief in the soul – the part of God in all living things

Avatar – 'One who descends' a Hindu god who descends to earth.

Awe – a feeling of great admiration or respect.

B

Baptism – a rite of initiation by immersing or sprinkling of water

Baptistry – the pool of water used by some Christians to initiate Believers' baptism

Belief – something you know to be real or true even though you cannot always prove it

Believers' Baptism – a Christian rite of initiation by fully immersing the body in water

Bible – the Christian holy book

Brahma – A Hindu god – one of the trimurti- considered to be the Creator.

Brahman – A Hindu name for God – the One Supreme Being

Buddha – A title given to Siddhartha Gautama, the founder of Buddhism – it means the 'Enlightened One'

C

Calligraphy – beautiful writing used as a form of art, especially by Muslims

Ceremony – special things said and done on formal occasions such as weddings

Christening – a Christian ceremony to give a baby its name and welcome them into the Christian family

Church – a Christian place of worship

Commitment – a strong belief in something shown by a promise to do something

Community – a group of people who share the same interests or beliefs

Confirmation – a ceremony to acknowledge a person's commitment to the Christian faith

Conversion – when a person changes to a different set of beliefs

Creed – a Christian statement of belief recited by many churches

Cremate – the burning of a dead body

Crematorium – a building where dead bodies are burned

Cross – a Christian symbol to represent the death and resurrection of Jesus

Custom – an activity that takes place on special occasions

D

Deity – The various forms and aspects of God in Hinduism

Denomination – a group within the Christian religion who may hold a particular point of view or belief

Dharma – the teachings of Buddha

Diversity – a wide variety of people, places, ideas and customs

Dukkha – a Buddhist belief in suffering and that life is unsatisfactory

E

Enlightenment – an understanding about what is true and real – the aim of all Buddhists

Environment – the natural world such as the land, sea, air and all creatures and plants

Evil – a wicked power that is opposed to God

F

Fard – what is obligatory or a duty according to Muslim law (Shari'ah)

Festival – a celebration of a religious event held every year

Five K's – symbols worn by Sikhs to express commitment to the Sikh faith

Five pillars – the five duties to be observed by Muslims

Font – the bowl which hold the water for baptism in a Christian church

Free Will – the idea that everybody is responsible for their own actions

G

Godparents – people who attend a baby's baptism and promise to bring the child up as a Christian

Gurdwara – the Sikh place of worship- also called a Temple

Guru Gobind Singh – The tenth and last Guru – the founder of the Khalsa

Guru Granth Sahib – The Sikh holy book

Keywords

H

Hadith – Sayings of the Prophet Muhammad

Hajj – pilgrimage to Makkah -the fifth pillar of Islam

Halal – what is permitted according to Muslim law (Shari'ah)

Haram – what is forbidden according to Muslim law (Shari'ah)

Heaven – the place where God is believed to be

Hell – the place where the wicked are punished

Hijab – a veil that Muslim women wear to cover the head.

Holy – something which is sacred or special

Holy Communion – a service using bread and wine that recalls the last meal that Jesus shared with his disciples. It is also known as Eucharist or the Lord's Supper

Holy Spirit – part of the Trinity. The Christian belief that God can reveal himself through divine energy

Hymn – a Christian song sung in praise of God

I

Infant baptism – a Christian ceremony to give a baby its name and welcome them into the Christian family – it involves the sprinkling of water

J

Jesus – Christians believe he is the Son of God – the founder of Christianity

K

Karma – a term used by Hindus, Sikhs and Buddhists to explain that all actions and thoughts affect a future rebirth.

Khalsa – a Sikh term meaning 'community of the Pure'

Kosher – means 'fit' or 'proper'. Food permitted by Jewish law

L

Last Rites – a religious ceremony carried out by a Christian priest before a person dies

Lectern – a reading desk or stand used for reading the Bible

M

Makkah – a holy city for Muslims and the place where Muhammad was born

Mandir – a Hindu place of worship – also called a Temple

Mass – a service using bread and wine practised by Roman Catholics

Meditate – to stay in a calm silent state of concentration for a period of time in order to think about something deeply

Mihrab – An alcove in the wall of a Mosque

Minaret – a tower at a Mosque from which the call to prayer (Adhan) is made

Minbar – a platform in a mosque where the imam(religious leader) gives the sermon

Minister – a member of the clergy in a Christian non-conformist Church

Moksha – the release of the atman (soul)

Monks – men who devote themselves to God by being a member of a religious community

Mosque – a Muslim place of worship

Mourner – a person who grieves for someone who has died

Mourning – an expression of sorrow and grief following the death of a person

Muhammad – Muslims believe he is the last messenger of Allah

Murti – the image or statue of a Hindu god

N

Nirvana – a Buddhist word to describe a state of perfect peace – the ultimate goal of Buddhists

Nuns – women who belong to a religious order and devote themselves to God or religion

O

Organic – naturally grown without outside help

P

Pacifist – a person who believes that war and violence are always wrong

Pilgrim – a person who makes a special journey to a religious place

Pilgrimage – a religious journey to a sacred place

Practices – something a person does regularly as part of their religion

Prashad – food that has been blessed and shared with worshippers

Precepts – guidelines or rules for Buddhist behaviour

Priest – a religious leader with special duties and responsibilities in a place of worship

Prophet – a messenger of God

Pulpit – a raised platform where a member of the clergy stands to preach their sermon in a Christian church

Puja – a Hindu term for worship